BEYOND

The Journey Towards Living and Feeling Life as a Whole Person

by

Richard Stone

BEYOND

The Journey Towards Living and Feeling Life as a Whole Person

Published by

R&E Publishers

P.O. Box 2008
Saratoga, CA 95070
Phone: (408) 866-6303
Fax: (408) 866-0825

I.S.B.N. 0-88247-863-X

Library of Congress 90-50894

Table of Contents

Preface

A friend—a good man with the willingness to question and raise doubts—read a draft of this text and said, "Something is missing. You need at least to write a preface. Tell what moved you to attempt this book, why someone should take the time to read it, how it should be read."

I guess it is not as evident as I supposed. The writing took place only because it demanded its existence. It was as if a guide directed, "Make use of what you've learned, turn the workings of that inquiring mind to account. Set forth your travels through, and more importantly, *beyond*, the society you were born into. Write of visits to various versions of hell, and to heightened states of consciousness. Extol the mundane as well as the exotic. Speak with equanimity about uncertainty, and with good humor about difficulties and failures. And, oh yes, suggest that moments of enlightenment can be experienced by anyone, though maintained by fewer than claim so.

But please, no autobiography!"

Thus a challenge was laid down. I warily took up the task and discovered a voice, low-key, logical, yet reconciled to paradox; a voice that allowed words and ideas to tumble forth in some order yet spontaneously, undogmatically. A manuscript was born.

Still, how to recommend it to others? A reader can't look in my direction and see a celebrated author, or someone of authoritative experience with a noteworthy institution. There is only a peripatetic soul that has made a modest success of achieving (and of necessity re-achieving) balance while encountering an abundance of unfamiliar cultures within and outside of American society. Having been led and drawn, pulled and pushed, into unexpected circumstances and disorienting frames of reference, my claim to attention is as one who can cope with Reality's incomprehensibility.

I see myself as someone able to guide others into an attitude where it is possible to question concepts and habits of thought that tend to shield us from the unknown; one able to lead mental excursions to places where the undomesticated nature of living can be glimpsed and paths into the wilderness be located.

In the writing, attention has been paid to addressing issues in practical, straightforward ways. Yet I see there may be a deception in this, as the book is not for those who want their idea of "what is" to remain simple. It is for those who can't accept easy answers for hard questions, for those who have an itch (if not a hunger) to enter into "the mystery of IT ALL." Perhaps above all, it is for people willing to accept that there is more out there than we know about, and it must be taken into account.

As for the reading itself, it is tempting to prescribe that each mental exercise or set of questions (with which the manuscript abounds) be taken as a necessary step in an orderly progression toward insight. My critic-friend even suggested a workbook format that would direct the reader literarily, if not literally, to construct the "room of mirrors" spoken of in the introduction.

The text can be used that way, and certainly I believe in the value of each thought experiment proposed. Then I remember: this material has been gathered over a twenty-year period. At any given time only small parts of it were of interest to me, or could even be taken in. Why should it be different for a reader?

More modestly, the book may serve as a spur to inquiry, to considering experience as a source of intelligence-making rather than a series of accomplishments. The particular questions posed are best taken as representative, not authoritative. They are definitely not rhetorical—I have, at some time in some way, wrangled with each one beneficially; and I would certainly encourage a reader to take any or all of them seriously, to enter into the inner discourse they tend toward. Yet I would be satisfied for a reader just to grasp the central concept of "the dialogue with the Other."

By this I mean, for example, that any statement I make about myself is both inclusive and exclusive. If I identify myself with a certain quality then (at least to an extent) I exclude the opposite. So, if I claim to be well-organized, then I downplay spontanaiety. How, then, do I relate to this "not me"? Do I devalue it? envy it? feel attracted, or repelled, by those who manifest it? When in contact with spontaneous people, do I respond predictably, or am I able to meet their anarchic tendencies constructively, freshly? Can I meet the unique circumstances of the particular situation?

The exploration of this kind of eternally changing relation to the Other is truly the basis of this work. The text is a way to make this process concrete, visible, familiar. So my hope is not that each chapter and each question be "done" doggedly, but that along the way some of the questions and experiments will take hold, will intrigue the reader to peek inside "the room of mirrors", and begin to entertain new images of life and living.

Fresno, 1990

Introduction

The Room of Mirrors

Living, like learning, is a process that has been sadly misrepresented by our society. With both, we are told there are right ways and wrong ways, things we should and should not do, things we should accomplish by a certain age if we are to be considered successful. With both, we are made to feel constantly graded (and often degraded) by external judges; and too often we begin to judge ourselves primarily by the standards of others.

With both living and learning, outside assistance is necessary—but also suspect. Others with more experience or more objectivity can tell us what we fail to see; can remind us that what seems a dead-end can be only a horizon; can encourage us to begin things which, without aid, seem overwhelming; and can help us concentrate on the value of each step along the way as well as the goal we have in mind.

We can also receive practical advice from others: which A's and B's are probably needed if we want to get to C; what skills are likely to come in handy in the future.

But each of us lives and learns in a unique way, and no one else is competent to judge what is enough or when we are ready for more—or for that matter, what the "more" should be.

This book is based on a journey of exploratory reflections I have undertaken over the years to make my own way through the maze of self-understanding. Each chapter represents a category of life, and the categories are necessarily arbitrary and over-lapping. But each, I believe, offers a useful point of reference, if the book's purpose is rightly understood. That purpose is, simply put, to assist readers in considering their lives in a whole way.

The word "whole" is related linguistically (and not incidentally) to the words "heal" and "well". My presumption is that in looking at our lives in a rounded and fair way, without pre-judging aspects as more or less valuable, we begin to heal ourselves, to find well-being.

I also presume that there is no all-encompassing method or system that puts it together for us, providing rules for all occasions. Instead, we seem to learn piecemeal, by taking each aspect on its own terms and enduring temporary contradiction. In some cases the paradoxes thrown up by this approach to understanding may suddenly resolve into a momentary "epiphany" of unifying insight. But there can be no successful epiphany-hunting, only living with as much honest consideration as possible for whatever presents itself to consciousness. The rest, it seems, is out of our hands.

My intent is to build a room of mirrors, so to speak, in which we can look at ourselves from all sides. Some angles are familiar and satisfying;

others may be strange, or unsettling, and these are the ones we need to look at most attentively.

Contemporary literature is filled with ideas and resources in most of the categories to be explored. In the text there are many references to branches of study, systems of belief or practice, organizations, and the like. I have benefitted from contact with all that are mentioned, and they are included as recommendations to a reader's attention.

My suggestion, though, is to enter gently and experimentally into contact with any of these resources. I also recommend that no matter how positive is the influence of experimentation in one aspect, a periodic glance around the whole mirror room would be beneficial. Even a slight experience with sculpting has taught me how important it is to keep turning the work and looking from all angles.

But, however it is done, there can be only gain. Failure doesn't exist here, only feelings of failure. Taken the right way, everything is grist for the learning mill. The room of mirrors is to be entered like a fun-house, for the sheer experience of it.

Part I: Private Life

I remember, as a youngster, wondering if the world disappeared when I shut my eyes; or if I died in my sleep, would I still be able to dream. When I was about 12 I learned the word "solipsism"—the belief that only the self exists or can be proven to exist. The thought that this may be true was fascinating, wonderful and horrible at the same time, resonating an inner hope of personal importance and a terrible fear of lonely responsibility.

I also remember hearing the mind-twister, "If a tree falls in the forest and nobody hears it, is there a sound?" I pondered this for hours without finding an answer that felt true.

Such puzzles must have teased into awareness elementary questions about self and one's place in Reality. Last year, rummaging among old papers, I found a poem written as a teenager. It had sprung forth, one solitary day, with no conscious precedent, beginning:

> "There is no great eternal Truth
> for Man to find or Man to lose
> But just a never-ending fire
> that constantly renews."

The "me" who wrote those lines had only the vaguest acquaintance with the boy who dutifully studied Latin and math, or the youngster who belonged to a Jewish Youth Group bowling league, or the misfit teen who tried in vain to imagine himself dancing on American Bandstand. The poignant mystery hovered ever near: isn't there any logic to living?

The chapters in this section are a return in spirit to considerations of the kind described above. They are intended to provoke investigation about living in one's skin, one's sensorium, one's mind, amidst the most intimate and personal "baggage" of personhood. Their subjects—identity, home and health—return to the basic questions of a developing consciousness, now to be re-examined from an adult's perspective.

One   Identity

From adolescence onward, most of us puzzle over the question, "Who am I?" This "I" is the subject of all kinds of sentences:

I think...

I feel...

I believe...

I want...

Yet there is also the confusing element of "I am supposed to think or feel or believe or want." And then comes the shocking discovery that the thoughts expressed in any or all of those sentences are challenged, or refuted by others, followed by the treacherous realization that what was thought to be "certain", "beyond question", "inevitable", is not.

My first year at summer camp, for example, as an innocent 8-year-old, I was eating and took some unchewable food from my mouth onto the plate. The counselor snapped at me about bad manners. I was startled, and began to defend myself by saying, "But my father does that at home," then choked the words back. An unformulated truth struck me silent: "I" was not my father. I was in a new situation, and, alone, had to find ways of living to suit the changed circumstances. "I" was part of a moving, changing tableau rather than being a fixed entity. My identity was shaken.

Isaac Deutscher relates a similar, more crucial incident in his autobiographical essay "The Non-Jewish Jew." Raised an orthodox Jew, a child prodigy who had mastered the Biblical studies required of a rabbi by his early teens, Deutscher (and everyone around him) considered his identity clear and his future laid out. But then, in an audacious youthful adventure, he and a friend slipped out of synagogue during Yom Kippur services. On the holiest, most solemn day of the Jewish year, they took it upon themselves to go to the cemetery and not only break the fast of the High Holy Day prematurely, but to eat meat and cheese (thus breaking the Kosher laws at the same time) in the presence of the revered souls of their ancestors.

They expected, at the very least, a lightening bolt to strike them down, humble their sacrilegious pride, subdue the devil driving them to such wickedness. But nothing happened...and Deutscher never went back to his rabbinic studies.

"I am not who I supposed. Who am I?"

Then again, there is the "me", the object of others' sentences. Parents, teachers, relatives, other people are constantly saying "You are this or that", be it smart or stupid, good or bad, polite or ungrateful. Who is this person they are talking about?

Did you ever look in the mirror and wonder, "If what appears there is 'me', who is it that is looking...and doesn't see itself?" What does it mean that you can't look your reflection in the eye, you can't see into your own soul as you can into others?

These awesome, precipitous questions of youth fade from mind for most of us as we enter adulthood. We make choices, adopt manners of living, settle into habits of thinking and acting and responding. We tend to become "personalities", recognizable, relatively predictable. Like Popeye, we say, "I am what I am."

It is my contention that *this very moment* is the time to pass beyond such certainty. At the very least, let us look at what makes up this "I" that claims such solidity. How did it come to its current form? what became of who it used to think it was? what can be said about its "me-ness" that seems to exclude so much yet is clung to so tenaciously?

The question, plainly put, is: "Which aspects of my living do I consciously identify with and take responsibility for?"

A good way to begin finding out is to write a list of completions for the sentence, "I am_____." At least ten answers should stretch the mind, more are welcome.

1. _____ 7. _____

2. _____ 8. _____

3. _____ 9. _____

4. _____ 10. _____

5. _____ 11. _____

6. _____ 12. _____

This list is a point of departure for self-examination. It may show at a glance certain emphases. For example, you can look at the balance between *attributes* (the qualities you possess, such as being kind, irritable, thoughtful, etc.) and *abilities* (the things you can do, such as being a mechanic, a student, an athlete.) Or you can compare *ascribed status* (being a woman, a son, a Catholic by birth) with *achieved status* (being a husband, friend, born-again Christian) resulting from your actions and choices.

Other dimensions can be added to the exercise by doing either or both of the following:

A. Go back to the list and rank each item as (1) "Of major importance" or (2) "Of lesser importance." Then think back to when you were half your age, and draw up a list for "I was _____." Look at the balances and ranking for that list, and then compare the two lists.

   What has been added, what replaced? What changes in emphasis have occurred? How do you see these changes? Do they seem natural and neutral? Are there things you regret having lost or feel proud to have attained? Do you see any trends that are cause for worry, or for satisfaction?

B. Ask a few people who know you well, preferably from differing contexts (such as home, work, interest group) and of both genders, to draw up lists about you (You are _____.) Do these lists confirm your own, or give you some things to think about? (If you're in contact with people who knew you in the past, their lists would be interesting, too.)

Next, I suggest that you scan the list of chapter headings for the remainder of the book. Mark those which seem of special interest or which are unrepresented in the lists you have previously drawn up. Here are the subjects:

—family and domestic life

—physical well-being

—social relations

—education

—work and social worth

—love and sex

—spirituality and psychology

—philosophy and the occult

Of those you've marked, which are you *prepared* to work on? (This is not the same as the most important one or the one you know you "should" do something about. It is asking instead which one most invites your attention and curiosity, which one seems accessible.) If you can select one, you may want to start there rather than at the beginning.

And bon voyage.

Two   Family & Domestic Life

For years there have been discussions about the disappearance of "community" in contemporary living. There are undoubtedly deficits in the mostly voluntary, and often "strictly business", nature of our social interactions. Yet there are probably as many advantages as losses in the change. After all, large numbers of people have fled the close-knit small-town life when given the chance.

In my thinking, the root issue is not community but home and family. By this I don't necessarily mean the nuclear family; the nostalgic (and often politically-inspired) exaltation of the nuclear family runs contrary to the facts and currents of real life. Still the power of this deeply-etched image remains, and its constraints must be overcome before we can look at the term "family" in its essentials.

I remember, for instance, my young cousin's bar mitzvah (Jewish coming-of-age ceremony), when his parents were called up to the altar to stand with him. As mother and father stood flanking their son, each with an arm around him, the sheer strength of that trinity sent tremors through me. Yet this response was countered at once by an instinctive shudder that only later found articulation. For I felt immediately that my unmarried, childless state excluded me from the force of that configuration in its literal form, and that the bonded stability of the family group might even pose a threat to me.

Then it came to me that I could participate in the strength of the family in other, less literal ways. I had already begun locating and interacting with the paternal, maternal and filial instincts within myself. Additionally, I could absorb (and learn from) the tableau I had seen...in fact, I recalled how past visits with my cousins had served to give me grounding at times when I was feeling lost.

Yet the other side of the question remained. Could those literally living out the familial symbol take *me* in and be reciprocally challenged? In some cases, including these particular cousins, the answer was "yes." In general, however, our society's idea of family still seems obstinately mired in the past, insisting that "family" be conceived of as a legal marriage, a wife and a husband, and children. For me, though, the question of family instead involves an inquiry into the existence of a base of operations. I could define family as *a network of relationships that provide sustenance and rightful belonging.* In short, family is whoever provides a true sense of home.

A good way someone can approach this area is to take a large piece of paper and a variety of drawing implements (crayons, markers, pastels, etc.) and create a pictorial representation of what your "family" is—however literal or metaphoric you want to be.

It is useful in doing this exercise to do it with others, as the range of responses can be surprising. If you are with others, look at each person's picture and notice the differences. You might comment on what you see in terms of color, order, variety, movement, emotive quality and the like; and ask questions about the intent of the drawer. (Avoid statements about what is lacking, even for your own.)

Turning to your picture, identify with every part of the picture, not just a particular figure or symbol. Speak about each part and its relation to other parts. When you've finished, try to articulate what you've confirmed and what you've discovered about this area of your life.

This exercise can give an impressionistic sense of the quality of your "home" life, and also broaden your notion of what is possible in this area.

Another way to approach this subject is to think about the key terms listed below. With each of them that strikes you as worth the effort, reflect on how it has appeared in your life.

baby	yard
older brother	plants/garden
older sister	neighbors
younger brother	neighborhood
younger sister	meals
twin/alter ego	playing
father	fighting
mother	tasks: maintenance, improvement
grandparents	hobbies
other adults	making decisions
pets	celebrating
house	spending free time
"my room"	spending money
living room	getting around (transportation)
kitchen	family atmosphere and system
bathroom	relatives and family friends
other rooms	being sick
furnishings	

You can play with these terms in a variety of ways, such as:

A) What did they used to mean to you as a youngster? How did you imagine they would turn out in later life? How do you see them now? (Allow your imagination loose rein, and include metaphoric associations, such as earth-mother or father of the country.)

B) Who or what sparked ideals, or provided models, or has lingered in memory for any of these terms? Have these models served you well, or proven inadequate in certain respects? Have you expressed your gratitude, ambivalence and/or displeasure? How do you regard these models now?

C) Has any of these terms been associated with a longing or emptiness in your life? Has that feeling slackened, or been satisfied, or put aside? Does that feeling ever recur in another context? How do you deal with it if it does?

You should now have generated a lot of information about what home means to you, what it has been and what it could be. Is there anything you feel impelled to change? What first steps can you take? Is there anything you want to celebrate? How might you do that?

Looking into the area of home and domestic relations can give you an idea of how strong, broad and coherent your primary survival resources are. It can show how connected you are to a system that provides assistance and guidance. It can show you the qualities of the support system you're associated with...its limitations and costs as well as its benefits.

Also, it can provide insight into the extent that life-experience has shaped your sense of relatedness to other people and your environment, that is, how far you have gone from your starting point. And it can offer some directions to move in if you want to change.

To go more deeply into this area, there are two kinds of resources I can suggest. The first set is investigative, a supplement to the exercises offered above. Here are a few of the many things that can stimulate your memory and imagination:

- family photographs

- memorabilia (diaries, letters, scrapbooks, etc.)

- paintings and art photos of family groups through history

- autobiographical writings or fiction about families

- greeting cards (your favored style may indicate your familial sentiments)

The second list of suggestions involves activity rather than contemplation, and is for those who feel enough dissatisfaction with this part of life that they want to do something about it.

For deep-seated problems, this area is the one most appropriate for conventional psychotherapy. The field has developed primarily around the study of individuals in the domestic setting. As is well known, Freud's system of analysis is centrally concerned with the internalized relationships of the child to Mother and Father, with how the child elaborates unconsciously (and often inappropriately) on its earliest domestic relationships as it passes through stages of sexual and social development.

Another related branch of therapy—family therapy—has focussed on how all the members of a (usually nuclear) family interact. It aims at identifying a more-or-less rigid "system" that has developed and is thwarting the individuals in some crucial way. This approach clarifies how those in close living connection affect each other in deep ways that most often they are only partly aware of.

Such therapeutic approaches can be very helpful if understood realistically. As a healing method, therapy is more akin to a program of slow rehabilitation than to the taking of an aspirin to relieve a headache; and as a learning process it is closer to learning Spanish because you're going to live in Spain rather than studying to pass a school exam.

If therapy is unavailable, unaffordable or uninviting, you can work on this area simply by involving yourself with aspects of it not now prominent in your domestic life. For example, if you are not in close contact with people your parents' age, or with the very elderly, or with young children, or with teenagers...and if the absence seems significant...you can do something that creates such contact. Most obviously, there are volunteer programs for assisting people of each age. Or perhaps you have relatives or neighbors you can involve yourself with.

You can also gain insight into your domestic life by paying attention to the physical environment of your home. Look at the colors, the materials, the style of furnishings. How were these chosen? Are they satisfying? What do they suggest about yourself?

Are individual needs for both privacy and togetherness being met? (You may want to take a survey on how each family member would like to arrange the available space.) How are meals arranged? How are TV shows decided on? How is free time spent?

Would the addition (or subtraction) of pets, of plants, of special equipment, make a difference? What changes can be made to bring sustaining connections among the people who share the space, to reduce feelings of threat or anxiety, to increase communication and caring.

What about the neighborhood? Have you made any effort to find out something about your neighbors, to explore possible connections with them? Have you tried how it feels to borrow things from them, or offer them things? Do you know if you share any personal interests, common needs (tools, babysitters, dentist) or neighborhood concerns (noise, traffic, etc.)?

Have you ever gone someplace with them or socialized with them? Have you made an effort to find communal interests—neighborhood watch, taking care of the street and trees, or the like?

The question is not whether it is possible (or desirable) to have a close-knit, friendly group of neighbors, but whether channels of communication have been opened and tested...and if not, why not?

Another aspect of neighborhood to consider is its diversity. To what extent are differences visible, be they ethnic, political, cultural or aesthetic? What balance between similarity and difference are you comfortable with? Is your individuality expressed—have you revealed alternatives to neighbors' choices or had yours challenged; and if so, what came of it?

Finally, what about a "home away from home"? Have you been to places that somehow gave you the feeling that you especially belonged there? Do you, for instance, sometimes long to run to the ocean, or the mountains, or the desert? Have you been some place that felt as if you'd finally come to the end of a long, arduous journey?

If you can, go to one of these special places (or recollect a visit). Pay close attention to the location's qualities, and how you respond to them. Do you feel like crying or laughing or singing? Do you feel reverent or exuberant or sensual? What seems to be providing inspiration, what seems to call for your deep participation?

Some time later, allow the experience to wash over you again as you reflect on your domicile. Can you imagine ways to bring something of that special place into your everyday life? Are there ways to bring in colors, sounds, textures, smells that echo your experience?

Behind this battery of exercises and questions lies the notion that "family" means more than spouse, children and a few close relatives. That there is a deeper sense of "home" beyond a residence that provides creature comfort and convenience. That by looking both at what exists matter-of-factly in our immediate lives, and at what has gained significance from our past (or from our imaginings) we begin a richly satisfying dialogue.

The ensuing chapters will pursue this dialogue into less familiar aspects of our lives.

Three Physical Well-Being

Our understanding of health has been changing recently from the definition of "absence of disease" to a more substantial model. Such aspects of physical status as vitality, balance, circulation, mobility, adaptability and resilience are commonly regarded as indices of health along with pulse, temperature, blood pressure, presence or absence of pain, swelling, secretions, and the like.

Gradually, people are learning to monitor their health in a more continuous way, with more awareness of what can signal the onset of difficulty. Still, the effect of the old biases remains. The new trend is often labeled "preventive medicine", and is thus defined as another kind of treatment (against future disease) rather than a process worth undertaking for itself.

But labels aside, millions of people are now informed about the value in paying attention to the quality and quantity of what they eat; exercising to keep limbs limber and the cardio-vascular system fully operative; knowing when, and how, to rest; respecting the intricate—and beautiful—*functioning* of the body as fully as its decorative aspects.

Our ability to monitor our own physical states is, however, seriously hampered by several influences. First, we live in an age that rejects tradition and seeks empirical "scientific" guidelines. Yet we are raised in utter ignorance of our physical components—how they work, what care they require, and especially the changes that occur through aging, use and abuse. (For example, if people saw clear illustrations of the effects of alcohol on the liver, or nicotine on the lungs, over a period of time, they might not be so attracted to drinking and smoking.)

Second, when alternative behaviors that may be beneficial to health are presented to the public, often they are turned into fads and extremes of activity that seem to require special clothes, consultation with experts, and measurable achievement. Jogging and aerobics, for instance, have become as much a way of dressing as of exercising, and have been tied to a goal-orientation that few feel adequate in or can long sustain.

Third, we tend to judge how well we are by comparison with how we usually feel. But our habitual states may not themselves be particularly healthy. How can we begin to get an objective assessment?

Certainly a thorough medical exam is a good place to begin. An exam need not be limited, though, to the kind given by an M.D. or hospital. For example, acupuncturists and homeopathic practitioners look for imbalances of subtle systems not recognized by western medicine. Chiropractors check the workings of the nervous system as it is affected by the alignment of the spine. And more prosaically, many YMCA's offer "fitness tests."

Second, we can spend time learning about the body—anatomy, the various systems such as respiratory and digestive, conditions related to the onset of disease or malfunction, aging, etc.

Third, we can familiarize ourselves with at least some of the maverick or non-western approaches to health subjects, such as are found in "natural health" magazines, chiropractic journals, the counter-culture press (such as Mother Jones Magazine), and the like.

One reason for such research is that conventional wisdom and common practice change, and it is good to be aware of the various factors that contribute to change. For example, the number of Caesarean births is reported to have dramatically increased in the last few decades: is this because fetuses are larger, or women less prepared for giving birth; or, as some maintain, is it because it is easier and more lucrative for hospitals to mechanize the procedure?

Similarly, questions about delivery practices are now being raised by proponents of natural childbirth, midwifery and home birth; by assertions by Dr. LeBoyer and others about the traumatic effect of hospital procedures on the newborn; by experiments with delivering infants in water. In ten years the "standard" way of delivery may well be very different than today's methods.

Other controversies abound concerning now-popular treatment modes. Do antibiotics destroy the balance of the immune system? What is the value of patent medicines such as antihystamines, cold suppressants, nasal sprays—what do they do and at what cost? Should the appendix—not to mention the uterus—be removed as readily as it has been? Should "heroic measures" to sustain life be used routinely?

It is important to realize that the institutions which provide "authoritative information" on such questions tend to acquire vested interests. These include financial interests, equipment outlays, established referral relations, the desire to preserve reputations, and the natural human tendency to hold on to one's belief system as long as possible.

Such interests make for an institutional resistance to new information. But we as individuals, lacking these vested interests, have no reason to insulate ourselves from new hypotheses and methods. We, not doctors, are responsible for our health, and it is up to each of us to find resources that give us freedom of inquiry; as much knowledge and choice as possible; and outcomes we can live, and die, with peaceably.

Thus, there is good reason to inform ourselves about alternative systems of treatment with different philosophies of treatment. Western medicine typically aims at suppressing symptoms and counter-attacking invasive organisms in a rather militaristic approach. It emphasizes isolation in a sterile environment (absence of germs, quarantine from everyday life, drug-induced reduction of thought and feeling, actual removal of tissue, etc.) It tends to be action-oriented and literal.

In contrast, there are systems which emphasize changing the inner state of the ill person. Such approaches include Chinese acupuncture and Japanese shiatsu; so-called "bodywork" based on the teachings of Wilhelm Reich, and the ancient practices of yoga and t'ai chi ch'uan; herb healing and Bach flower remedies; the use of music, quartz crystals and healing energies. (Chapter 9) All these involve close personal attention by the health practitioner, responding to minute bodily manifestations of stress. They aim at calming (rather than flattening) the mind and spirit through soothing attention and subtle stimulation, redressing imbalances in the patient's state of being that have prevented self-healing from occurring.

In question here are sharp differences in what is viewed as available for treatment, and how change is looked at. If I understand myself as a mechanical system, I will look for a "repair man" to make a mechanical intervention. If I understand myself as part of God's plan, I will look for intervention by way of prayer. If I view myself as part of a complex of chemical and biological processes, I will look for ingredients to alter those processes. And so on.

But this book's basic premise is that there is no one way for us to conceptualize ourselves, and that what is most helpful is to entertain several perspectives even when they seem contradictory. We then have access to several approaches to healing, and we are free to use whatever works, whichever practitioners we trust. For when all is said and done, belief and trust are probably the central factors in healing.

Another interesting fact of language: we typically speak of "getting better" after an illness—a comparative state that indicates we are again able to function. This phrasing suggests impatience and lack of attention to attaining full health. We don't care about getting well, but about getting back to our routines...though often the routines themselves are health-impairing.

Human life encompasses millions of minor miracles of adaptability, courage and endurance under stress. Taking advantage of this range, we have exerted our physical and mental faculties to an extreme in order to achieve a kind of material progress. But despite our newly-acquired mechanical ease in a variety of activities, many people have started to question this direction, as they find themselves without confidence in their true well-being. Many find themselves in fear of disease, accident, environmental poisoning, nuclear warfare, economic displacement, aging, and death.

If we begin to consider that our social system may itself be out of balance, we need to find gauges of health outside our ability, or occasion, to adapt to that system. Toward this end, close analysis of our basic biological systems may prove helpful. We can look at our respiratory system; our patterns of eating, digesting and eliminating; our success in getting sleep and rest; our sexual and creative energies; our maturation process.

Here, in detail, is an approach to one of these systems, eating. Eating may once have been simple. An organism took in amounts (regulated by an automatic system that said "enough") of what was available from the list of substances its genes and early training indicated to be edible.

Many organisms are, in fact, programmed in their eating. Some ingest only occasionally, others in a continuous, rapid cycle of intake and excretion. But humans are not so programmed. Traditional cultures established widely diverse eating patterns according to circumstance. Then, as cultures increasingly lost the limiting factors that shaped them, as their work and domestic patterns were altered, as the availability of a variety of foods increased, the bases of choice and timing for eating lost traditional moorings. As with so many other areas of life, we are now called on to use our own judgment—or be left at the mercy of the judgments of others much less attuned to our needs.

One important factor in looking at our eating habits is that, for humans, eating is often used for purposes other than hunger or nutritional needs. Eating reinforces communal bonds; serves as a ritual taking-in of strength or giving up one's due; serves as reward and punishment ("If you clean up, I'll give you a cookie" vs. the prisoner's proverbial bread and water); is used to celebrate anniversaries, successes, commeraderie; provides emotional reassurance; indicates status and wealth.

None of these purposes is "bad". They can, though, be confusing, and can pose health problems when they are not carried through with consciousness of the entire eating cycle, which includes digestion, utilization of intake, and elimination.

Some questions to think about when determining if there is an eating problem:

1. Do you spend more time than you'd like to, or than seems reasonable, thinking about food?

2. Are most food choices made without reference to nutritional needs, without knowledge of the value or disvalue of eating particular things in given quantities?

3. Is your body weight, or distribution of weight, a source of concern as a result of your diet? Has your fat level been found to be too high by an objective test such as a calipers test?

4. Do you often feel hungry or thirsty? (If yes, have you tried to find exactly which, and how much, of certain foods helps assuage these needs over time? Might you have psychological hungers for things other than food—rest, companionship, physical contact, caring attention—that eating is used to substitute for?)

5. Do you have trouble digesting what you take in? Do you have frequent upsets, or rely on digestive aids?

6. Do you not eliminate wastes in a fairly regular way, without much attention or dosing needed? Do bowel movements feel complete, as if you've been fully purged?

7. Do you have trouble choosing what and when to eat? Do you often feel cheated, or that you had the wrong thing? Do you tend to want everything, and not have preferences at given times? Do you never feel full, or know that you don't want to eat more? Is it hard to leave something uneaten on the plate, to throw excess food away or save leftovers for another time?

If there is a pattern of yesses to your answers, you may want to explore this area in greater depth. Exploring does not mean finding another diet-and-exercise plan. It means giving close attention to food choices, and to how decisions about eating/not eating are made. It means trying out new approaches. And it means relocating a stable, trustworthy "command center" for food-related activities.

There are books that can help in this process.** Also, support groups such as Weight Watchers or Overeaters Anonymous can be useful in restoring a sense of order and confidence in making food choices. But it is important to realize that the group approach tends to neglect the individual

----

**Some old favorites:

Overweight: causes, cost and control by Jean Mayer (Prentice Hall, 1968)
Anti-diet by Lynn Donovan (Nash Publications, 1971)
Psychologist's Eat Anything Diet by Leonard and Lilian Pearson (P.H. Wyden, 1973)

dynamics of preference and desire. An emphasis on the external goals of intake limitation and weight maintenance tends to turn into a cut-and-dried regimen or an on-going test of self-discipline. Less directive approaches aimed at bringing heightened awareness and informed intelligence to bear on the matter are at least of equal importance. It seems healthier to understand how best to include eating in our lives than to treat food as an enemy that we have to guard against.

Food is, of course, just one of several "inputs" into our system. We take in air, bacteria, sound and light; all kinds of electrical and chemical waves, particles, impulses. We are exposed to ideas, emotions, direct and indirect persuasions. Likewise, we transmit the same.

Just as we looked at our food intake-output system, we can examine the quantity and quality of what we take in and put out in these other areas. We can find out about the light, air, water, sound in our environment, and examine their effect on us. We can (notably in various kinds of structured interpersonal group processes) receive objective information on how we are affected by other people, and how we tend to affect them. We can be sensitized to how we receive, process, transform and communicate various kinds of energy. (This latter endeavor includes attention to our freedom and blockages in such things as breathing; posture and movement habits; acuity of the senses, including the intuitive and psychic; creativity and expressiveness in everyday living; sexual and physical vigor.)

We can also look into our health maintenance, e.g., how we treat our various systems. Do we know how to take care of our limbs, our organs, our senses, our mind? Do we give them rest, or work them continuously?

Do we give them sabbaths and vacations? Do we cleanse them, check their connections and contact points, give them TLC? Do we feed them, do we let them play as well as work?

More specifically, we can look at our ability to breathe and sweat freely; the condition of our nasal and bronchial passages; feelings of stress and tension; disturbances of sleeping and dreaming; lack of flexibility and agility in our limbs; recurring pains; lack of interest and affection; unawareness of the constant changes in living that call for re-orienting our responses in each new situation.

This kind of home-made checklist can indicate one's current state of well-being. But in thinking about "health", I begin to understand it more broadly as the focus of a personal reconciliation of mind with matter, of individuality with the environment. Our "self" is our truest, most independent domain, but a healthy self is not defined by wholeness of the individual body and mind.

After all, we are always decaying and regenerating, and physical life is defined by mortality, by birth and death. Our senses, too, are naturally limited. We are literally blind and deaf to things that other species can detect, as well as figuratively insensate in regard to much of what we register unconsciously. Our abilities to move and be moved, to perceive and respond effectively—to achieve conscious understanding and perform adequately—are all imperfect. It is only when our impairment is worse than usual that we notice.

Moreover, we are constantly subjected to conditions that change the framework within which our consciousness tries to achieve balance. So feelings of health may be largely related to how we deal with these changes, and with the shifts in attention and activity they require.

Health, then, can be seen not as a state but as an *attitude* that enables us to transform experience into learning and improving the quality of life. It would, as such, involve collecting information, performing acts of dutiful care, observing balances, allowing freedom, and (perhaps hardest for us to accept) acquiescing to a certain degree of suffering. In this perspective, ill health is a disruption of routine that demands adaptation and the examination of our habits...not warfare.

Signs of illness—such as fever, pain, paralysis, etc.—require attention and response. But as we consider the great number of organisms, qualities, impulses, energies that co-exist within (or pass through) our physical bodies, each with its own rhythms and directions; and as we take into account the many systems that involve or impinge on us, it is not easy to know how to respond. What interventions should be made? What re-alignments or re-organizations will be beneficial? What forces should we give way to, which should we challenge? In this perspective, it seems clear that there is a person, not an illness, to be treated.

Health, then, becomes a relative term. It is a measure of the suitable fitting of a being to all its purposes, of an individual to the forces of the Universe. Perhaps we can re-state our basic question about health in this way: do we know what is involved in the living, and dying, of our organism in its current environment? Do we recognize—and *accept*—the probable consequences of continuing to behave the way we do?

The hallmarks of good health would then seem to involve a broad understanding of the elements of life; adaptability to changing circumstances; and the ability to discover or invent appropriate ways to re-establish stability.

Part II: Involvement with Society

To be human is to be social. As behavior in our evolving species became less programmed to reflex, the amount of influence given to the social environment increased. A child's impulses to develop its potentiality for movement, speech and other necessary activities came more and more to be guided by the example of other humans. So now, our capacities are developed largely in imitation of and in response to the particular people and social activities around us.

Sometimes in the light of a society's miserable circumstances, it may be tempting to want to start all over again. In fact, the American experience was originally conceived this way, as an escape from the corruption of "Old World" culture. But once inside a social circuit, there is no ready way out. Even should we remove ourselves to Nature and commune in splendid isolation, it would take years of work even approximately to empty ourselves of socially-instilled perception. We would, for example, have to learn to think without reference to the paraphernalia of culture, respond without inclusion of memory.

But while there is undoubted value in gaining a measure of detachment from life's surface forms in antidote to the literalism and materialism of our education, why deny the power of socialization? In fact, if this book has a motto, it is, "Enter in whole-heartedly and intelligently," not "Escape."

From this perspective, the aim of this section is to suggest approaches to social involvement that invite participation, but on different terms than usual.

Four Social Relations

We are born within the realm of a dominant social group, a dominant ideology. In some way we must each come to terms with that society—to find a way to deal with its values, demands, models, opportunities, restrictions.

Yet in our age of very complex self-study, our social identities typically are broken into an array of sub-groupings. These include belonging to (or not belong to) status groups determined by external facts (income, age, urban or rural habitat, gender, ethnicity, I.Q., marital status, occupation, etc.) Some of these may be changed or modified by choice (e.g., relocating, having children, changing religious affiliation) or as a by-product of life (growing older, becoming disabled, losing a job.)

As a result of this complexity, we are all faced with a number of situations that leave us identified as both social majorities and minorities, each of which may lend vastly differing degrees of influence and esteem or powerlessness and oppression. Some of these "belongings" we are proud of, others may embarrass us; but they are all part of who we are.

The issue to be grappled with here is how to form principles of social relationship that take the "whole person" into account, not just those aspects of self that provide reassurance and a sense of self-righteousness. Bluntly put, how do we relate to being part of, rather than in control of, the social process? How do we relate to limitations on our personal power?

A prominent case concerns children. We tend naturally to value children as the guarantors of social continuity. We may well be attracted to them for their vivacity, curiosity, openness...and for the chance they seem to offer for recovering our own lost innocence. We may respond instinctively to their obvious need for help in receiving basic needs (shelter, nourishment, loving attention, stimulation, etc.)

Nevertheless, in political terms, children are virtually powerless. We like to believe that the decisions we make for and about them are for their own good, which we know better than they do. And of course, children cannot know all the relevant circumstances and likely consequences of certain decisions: they need our guidance. Nevertheless, when we as adults are involved in decisions about children, we often act in especially emotional ways ourselves...often based on notions about childhood derived unreflectingly from our own early experiences. It is exceptionally difficult for us to grasp differences in the circumstances children grow up in today, and to understand the needs of individual children with specific aptitudes, weaknesses, sensitivities.

In our actions regarding children, where we exercise so much power and responsibility, it seems crucial to develop a degree of objectivity with which to evaluate and respond to issues.

We can begin, in fact, with the issue of childbearing itself. If we take as our base that nothing is to be valued in isolation, then the creation of offspring begs to be considered in the larger context of maintaining planetary health. It is relevant to ask such questions as: How many children can I raise in physical health and mental well-being? Does my particular society seem over- or under-populated? Are the demands of the human population in general endangering the existence of other species and the natural environment which contribute to our life-support system?

Each of these questions is open to lengthy debate. The last, for instance, is a question posed by ecologists who created a scientific discipline in large part in response to evidence that human society has erred badly in its relations to the rest of nature. Ecologists look at all elements of nature as being inter-dependent. From their perspective, human society seems to have pursued technological achievement without sufficient regard to our own biological connections. We have not given adequate attention to the needs of the animals and plants, the air, water and soil that we co-exist with, and which life depends on. Moreover, we seem to have done this without purposeful intent, without understanding the probably consequences or implied judgments of our actions.

As we find out, for example, about the effects of chemicals and nuclear by-products—many of which can alter organisms and the environment in unknown ways for centuries—at very least we must emerge from naivete and accept responsibility for our decisions. And these decisions take us right back to the children: our radiation and pollution will affect the health and genes of the children in negative and possibly disastrous ways well beyond the lifetimes of today's adults. If our current rate of reproduction demands this new technology, we would seem to be caught in a self-destructive imbalance.

Here again is the question, "How many children can we raise well?" and here come those troublesome issues of birth control and abortion. To my mind, it is not so important to be on one or the other side in these debates as to understand the ground of discussion. The essence, as I see it, is an attempt to find ways of expressing a love of life, an alliance with the power of creation.

The chief elements to consider would seem to be these: 1) While food supplies and medical advances have improved, offering the possibility of prolonged life to more humans, so has the equal right to decent existence become a generally accepted human demand. 2) Yet, as we grant individuals the right to "more", we come into contact with the limits of ecological balance and of our conventional methods of distributing goods. 3) The rights of the unborn are to be defended (both in terms of being allowed birth, and in terms of being born into a tolerable environment) but so too must the sanity and well-being of the already living be honored. 4) Sex as a procreative activity is balanced by sex as a mode of communication and a therapeutic recreation: the value of each aspect deserves its due (cf. Chapter 7).

The fate of children rests on decisions respecting all of these issues. My point is that being socially responsible requires more than an emotional response. It is short-sighted to become fervid about one of such inter-locking questions without attending to the others. At the very least, if personal feelings or beliefs bring us passionately to one or another ideological party, we can still respect the intelligence and integrity of others who are swayed by different considerations.

One other point to be gathered from this discussion: social involvement through children is not synonymous with "having" children. One can actively concern oneself with issues of education, the quality of the environment, population size, disarmament, or the like, with specific consideration of the effects on children. One can defend the rights of children, who are without political power of their own. In contrast, one can pro-generate without being deeply drawn into "the fate of children."

Similarly, an important though difficult fact to grasp is that childhood is not just a stage we grow out of on the way to maturity. It is *a way of understanding* all its own, and its status in our communal thinking reveals much about the development of our conscience and consciousness. The consideration we accord children (and their perceptions), the quality of time given to them on their terms, is a critical index of the quality of our involvement with society as a whole.

For our dealings with children in fact parallel our relations with others who do not fall into categories of high social status or recognized capacity: those with some form of abnormality (be it physical, mental, emotional or behavioral); the elderly; minorities not yet incorporated into social legitimacy such as "illegal aliens", socialists, homosexuals, atheists.

In all these cases, we are dealing with aspects of ourselves. We all will have times of enfeeblement or ineptitude. We all have impulses and desires—we are impelled to actions—that are not socially approved. We all at some time hold beliefs that put us at odds with those around us. In short we all experience minority or disfavored status. So when we are face-to-face with people who cannot disguise or gloss over such qualities in themselves, but take them on (voluntarily or not) as a significant, enduring and public part of their identity, we confront a feared and often frightened part of ourselves. The way we enter into these encounters tells us about our interest in, our compassion for, our strength to deal with ourselves as much as with others.

Just as with children, we participate in making decisions that concern politically powerless underlings and outsiders. It is of vital importance that we explore our relations with them deeply enough to make conscious choices that we accept responsibility for.

Here is one of the most awesome challenges of social living. It is the opportunity given us to help redeem the neglected, underdeveloped—even despised—parts of the human psyche in our own time, rather than bequeathing the problems to the next generation.

Five   Education

After many years spent as "a teacher", working with people of diverse ages and capabilities, I am certain that education means something quite different than "going to school." To paraphrase John Dewey, education is the on-going process of learning from experience. It has no specific content, and it is unique for each individual. Ultimately, we each must educate ourselves, and take responsibility for our own learning.

As stated in the previous chapter, I do believe that adults have important educational responsibilities to children. I have grave doubts, however, if schools as we know them are the best place for most of these responsibilities to be acquitted. If nothing else, the adult/child ratio leaves little possibility for more than highly directed, "disciplined", activity. In addition, though, schools over-value written, easily testable "knowledge", and emphasize activities that may possibly have training value for the future (e.g. sitting all day at a desk) but have no relation to the expression of the youngster's current living interests and pressing concerns.

Schooling serves some purpose, but it is a terrible mistake to equate it with education. Recently I have questioned many acquaintances about their own learning process. "What," I asked in a structured interview, "were the key institutions, individuals, ideas, encounters that shaped your beliefs and gave you direction?"

To my lack of surprise, very few gave more than a passing reference to school, and then as often as a negative as a positive influence. Those who benefited often indicated that school was where they learned basic academic skills (but many learned these elsewhere) and that significant learning usually occurred in the first couple of grades. Some indicated appreciation for a quiet, structured environment—often when home was hellish—and for the opportunity to meet and mingle with peers. Some mentioned particular teachers. None felt that prolonged schooling was particularly beneficial, and most indicated that their important learning experiences took place by self-initiated activities and chance encounters (in or out of school.)

The point here is not to dismiss schools, but to demonstrate that they are only one source of learning, and in general are more important for their social than for their academic offerings.

The responses to the questionnaire reinforced my basic presumptions about education. In my view, education is not a fixed curriculum, nor a passage up rungs of a ladder to a degree; not an enterprise carried out in mandatory classes arranged to "cover" certain material; not obedient behavior.

Education, to the contrary, involves learning to live expressively and skillfully in the wide variety of situations invented by our growing up. To the extent that preparation for this adventure is society's responsibility, education means introducing young initiates to the range of society's possibilities. In this light, good education entails the involvement of children with a number of adults possessing greatly differing skills and interests, and admittance of children into as many of society's activities as possible as early as feasible.

As stated earlier, most human behaviors (from speech, to use of limbs in manipulating the artifacts of everyday life, to appropriate emotional expressions) are innately possible but do not become part of the individual's repertoire without example and practice. Adults need to provide environments and occasions where activities can be observed and tried. As children enter the age of physical readiness for specific learning, they need elders to help them develop a) an experimental attitude toward new behavior, b) physical and mental coordination, c) habits of practice and attention to detail, and d) the chance to use new skills in unstructured but unhazardous situations.

Secondly it is up to adults to demonstrate the need to take care of things—from cleaning and maintaining one's body, to caring for clothes and possessions, to raising plants or pets. Children can also gain awareness from adults of how actions affect others: if I throw gum on the street, someone else may step in it; if someone else throws the gum, I may step in it.

Thirdly, adults model behavior that implies values—what are priorities in life, how to act under stress or when challenged, how to make decisions and resolve disputes, how to keep self-respect and still recognize the rights of others.

Fourth, adults can help children place themselves in the universe. In part this means providing youngsters with information about their background (e.g. their extended family with its religious and ethnic traditions); about personal knowledge of neighborhood and locality, including geography, history, social make-up and changes, flora and fauna, etc. It also means providing them with information about, and exposure to, others from as wide a variety of backgrounds as possible.

Fifth, and perhaps most in need of implementation, adults can provide children with respect, and as much freedom as is consonant with safety and the available resources. In other words, adults can give their time and attention to protecting and guiding children in the children's self-selected activities. This is not teaching, it is not superimposing adult goals or knowledge on children or acting as master of a craft: it is, rather, *being* with children. And it is important that children's time with adults be spent in many environments, as children need to explore and become familiar with the range of society's habitats, be they stores and businesses, clinics and rest homes, parks and cultural centers.

Only education of this kind enables a true "next generation" to unroll from its predecessor. But if we limit our understanding of society to only what already exists, we value our own ideas and activities almost exclusively. So, sad to say, our society's priority-setting does not normally allow children to develop individually and responsively. We herd children into ghettoes called schools with an insufficient number of adults to supervise them.   This situation, of course, necessitates regulated, "disciplined" activities conducive to either passivity or rebellion, not learning. For this reason, any adult time spent with children in a free setting is a very important contribution to the next generation, as is time spent working to free children from the oppression of a regimented, stigmatizing school system.

To evaluate our own participation in the responsibilities of such an educational ideal, it is not enough to look at how active we are in the PTA, in attending our children's classes or helping them with homework. We need also to ask ourselves such questions as:

— Do we find out from children (our own and/or others') what is on their minds, what and how they are learning...not just in school? Do we spend time entering their world of activity and interests, and do we take their concerns seriously?

— Do we allow children to know how we spend our time, what is of interest and importance to us? Do we allow them to enter into our activities? Do we tell them our histories, and how we came to be as we are and to do as we do now?

— Do we introduce children to a variety of cultures and ideas?

— Do we show that we, too, are learners, without all the answers? Do we respect the interests and tastes of others? Do we exhibit curiosity about life, try the unfamiliar, attempt activities we may not excel (or even be good) at?

These questions are directed at examining the learning models we demonstrate to children as well as the extent of our educational involvement. At the same time, they are meant to suggest the importance of continued learning in our own lives, in or out of school. If we consider learning as a natural, essential activity like eating and sleeping, the issue becomes not *whether* we remain involved in education, but *how*: how apt we are as learners, how responsible and responsive we are as teachers.

After all, any experience can become a learning experience. How does an individual structure his or her living? how do facts and impressions and rhythms and ideas combine into satisfying or unfortunate experiences? In presenting our own responses to others (either formally or simply by expressive "being"), are we not, in effect, serving others as teachers?

Or, to dig a bit deeper, must we inhabit a world perceived as pre-determined, whose laws and principles we must single-mindedly strive to learn and obey? Is our lot solely to adjust to an unambiguous "given"; and having found a niche in that inexorably organized world, to cling to it till death? Is our educational function only to absorb as children, and re-indoctrinate as adults?

Or, can we see the world which we belong to as "intelligent", the locus of fresh understanding and creativity? Can we continue throughout life to participate in intelligence-producing activities—the gathering and dissemination of a flow of *mindful* information and responses?

Can we treat others (children, strangers, non-human life forms) as similarly participating in this universal intelligence, worthy of interaction and exchange? Do we make efforts to discover the common language, the hidden pathways, that allow communication?

This alternative understanding of education helps explain why we may welcome artists and spiritual philosophers into our lives. They are guides who induce us to glimpse the movement, hear the thoughts, of what we previously mistook as dumb and inert.

If we do not enter the river of ever-flowing learning, we confine ourselves to the functions of reproducing and dying. But if we can take to heart our intuitive knowledge that children represent the hope of the world, then another possibility opens to us. By honoring and trusting their redemptive innocence, while taking on the real responsibility of educating them to the world they live in, then we, too, enter into the process of self-renewing creativity and Creation.

Six   Work and Social Worth

I work. That means I engage my energies in seeking sustenance. I use my intelligence and inner resources in creating appropriate responses to the circumstances I am enmeshed in. I strive in the service of ideas and institutions that benefit myself and others.

Our sense of worth is related in large measure, for most of us, to our success in work. We typically interpret this to mean our involvement in "productive activity" which provides us access to social assets—notably material goods, power and respect. To judge our social worth accurately, however, we need to go beyond the gross notion of "job" and "income" so readily used in this country.

As feminists have ably demonstrated, the value (and even the definition) of "job" has been discriminatory. Occupations involving everyday maintenance are valued less than those directly involved with technical accomplishment or material production. Occupations dealing with children are "worth" less than those dealing with adults. Working for the wealthy counts for more than for the poor. Intellectual labor has higher status than work with an emphasis on nurturance and emotional resources. Moreover, time spent in activity aimed at making money is self-justifying, while time spent for less tangible rewards is subject to question.

Home-making, of course, epitomizes these biases. Sixteen hours a day can be spent at it, but it is still not considered a job. It is a status, a state of life, a fate. Many other occupations (typically those viewed as women's work, such as teaching, nursing, secretarial work) have been little more till recently.

What I wish to look at here is not "job", with its socially defined connotations, but the quantity and quality of socially productive work that one does. Some components of social utility to look at are:

1) **Benefit:** Do my activities (and not just their products!) contribute beauty, order, freedom, well-being, refreshment, intellectual stimulation, moral courage to others? It is important here to look at the net effect of activities rather than just their overt intent. A doctor's condescending attitude or carelessness may bring about an overall decrease in a patient's well-being. A shop clerk's courtesy may be a great gift.

2) **Effectiveness:** How many circles do my activities reach—family, neighbors, friends, special interest groups, a local population, a wider populus? How deeply does my work affect others—does it touch their material lives alone, or also their general ability to function, their minds or spirits? Is its impact brief or long-lasting, incidental or structural (i.e. does it change the way people organize and think about their lives?)

3) **Completeness:** We all work within a chain or system of related activities. Even an artist creating alone needs his or her work displayed, publicized, considered in a context. The question raised is, how fully do I feel integrated into the larger process I work

within? Do I know more, am I capable of more, than my defined task allows me to demonstrate? Am I permitted to learn and to expand my responsibilities? Do I understand, approve of, trust the decisions made around my work...or at least feel confident that my views and values are taken into account? In a broader perspective, do I feel that the process I'm part of is worthy of my time and attention? Have I thought through the impact of this process on society—in what ways is it beneficial and in what ways does it feed injustice, wastefulness, exploitation? Does this "work" address what I believe to be important, or at least allow scope to express my beliefs within the work setting? Or do I segregate my sense of social involvement from my job—in the classical terms of Karl Marx, am I "alienated from my labor?"

There are likely to be contradictions in the answers to these questions. I still have very mixed feelings, for instance, about a year spent working as an administrative clerk at a public agency. At first, there was the challenge of learning complex tasks and performing them with required efficiency. Also there was room for me to develop a few new procedures, and a decent mix of paper work and people contact, sitting and moving, working alone and as part of a team.

I felt the agency's goals (providing housing assistance to low-income families) were worthwhile, and were planned to minimize dependency. The administrative hierarchy was spotty, but had enough intelligence and managerial skill scattered around to make life bearable. And the "office pool" I worked with was the real joy of the job—hard-working, cooperative, full of little surprises and human touches.

Yet despite the good things, ultimately the job was not right for me. Partly, it took so much out of me that I couldn't attend to other projects that had impelling importance. Partly it was the daily grind of a bureaucracy, where the work was judged statistically rather than personally, where the emphasis was on keeping the process smooth rather than engaging with the people we encountered. It was readily felt that our function was basically mechanical, although we were able to humanize it somewhat through our own initiative.

The uneasiness also came in recognizing that I, too, was considered foremost as a mechanical part of the process. An organization had been developed, according to established concepts which required human agents to carry them out. Although the agency was relatively humane, it was founded on a production model that created a subtle but deepening rift between my sense of what is important in life and the way the agency directors required me to live half my waking hours. When I left the job I was confused about what to next, but what a relief to be out of a false situation!

This experience confirmed for me the complexity of the notion of "work." It showed the difficulty in discovering a true *life-task*, and not being seduced by a job taken for legitimate work-related reasons such as providing service, participating in a larger-than-self project, and earning a livelihood.

In this analysis I have skirted around the last of those topics because I do not feel secure in how to approach it, and have not been especially successful at it in my own life. Still I do have some tentative notions to put forth and (of course) some questions.

In thinking about this topic (which can be alternatively formulated as "supporting myself and my dependents", "making money", or "getting what I need and deserve from life"), I want to differentiate some related terms. *Work*, in my thinking, means any sustained effort to achieve desired goals. Only to the extent that an activity is whole-heartedly dedicated to a personally valued goal, or is at least held in renewed relation to such a goal, would I call it "my work" or a *vocation*.

In contrast, we may become caught up in routine tasks in order to sustain ourselves in an established way of life. Time so spent I term an *occupation*—valuable perhaps to others, but not a true calling. Or we may do something without direct relation to our goals in order indirectly to further their progress, such as take a job to earn money to live on or further a cause. To the job we contribute *labor*, but not our full intelligence or deeper selves.

A distinguishing feature of doing "my work" is that, as the old saying goes, it is its own reward. It is done from a deep necessity, from knowledge of what existence calls on us to do. Its main compensation is satisfaction for doing it well, and it is a bonus to receive recognition (whether it be thanks, or gifts, or even the mixed blessings of fortune and fame) from others.

It is my belief, something I try to live by but cannot prove (and, to be candid, sometimes doubt) that to the extent that we identify our true work, and root it deeply in social involvement, to that extent our livelihood will take care of itself. We will be placed surely in Life's current in which ebb and flow, income and expense, are approximately equal. But (as one of the Rolling Stones' songs puts it) in these matters we get what we need, not what we want. Payment may be in kind, not cash; and life, not a particular lifestyle, is what is supported.

Also, it may not be easy to locate your calling. Sometimes we are "out of grace" so to speak—out of the Garden—and we must labor. We may lose patience with the search for a vocation; we may feel pressed to secure material existence at a certain level for ourselves and dependents. We may find ourselves on a path—a career—that others have laid out for us. We are conscripted by circumstance into the armies of the wage-slave. In such cases, a different set of problems awaits us.

First comes the question of remuneration for labor. Is it fair? Is it representative of what the labor contributes to the enterprise—in terms of what the enterprise brings in, in terms of what other employees contribute and earn, in terms of what people doing comparable work make elsewhere?

Such questions come naturally to those at the bottom rungs of the employment ladder, but they are equally valid for upscale folk. Professional (lawyers, M.B.A.'s, entertainers, sports figures, and the like) are often paid according to the vagaries of a competitive market, in accord with projections of short-term profit rather than long-range social worth. For them to build an understanding of themselves and their place in the world on inflated salaries can be as destructive as for someone to judge him- or herself as inferior simply on the basis of low income.

In fact, one piece of personal work we each have is to understand the degree of prosperity or poverty we are born into, live with, fall into, attain. If we ask at all, we tend to ask ourselves questions like, what does it mean that I (or my family) is so rich or so poor? why don't I prosper like another, or why am I exempt from economic struggle?

But the ready-made answers to these questions, offered by religious and social moralities, tend to be contradictory. We still hear refrains of the old Christian warning that wealth is a sign of corruption; and of Jesus' words that the rich man can get to heaven about as easily as a camel can go through the eye of a needle. We've also inherited the Jewish belief that a people's oppression and poverty are due to its sinfulness, and the Protestant creed that prosperity is a sign of God's blessing. We are influenced, too, by the ideology that material success indicates "fitness" and superiority—the right to power. While in contrast, there's also the democratic dogma that everyone has an equal right to material well-being.

I suspect that the way out of this maze is to ask a different set of questions based on a somewhat different set of presumptions, with a less materialistic understanding of well-being.

It is certainly valuable to look at factors contributing to one's native estate and to gain insight into the attitudes and actions that have been important in determining it. Here is is useful to understand the costs and losses of certain choices, of certain emphases that one's self, family, race and nation have made. But perhaps more important is sensing deeply how our material status colors our relations to others, our capacity to know "reality" and act responsively in that knowledge.

Relevant questions in this sphere are: How does my standard of living compare with others not only in my society but in other societies as well? What do I need more of—food, health care, shelter, space, time? What do

I have enough of? more than enough of? What intangibles do I lack (such as peace of mind, safety, sense of well-being) that I would trade some of my material surplus for?

Or, in another perspective, how does my material status affect the way I think about myself? Does it give me a sense of power, or make me feel at a disadvantage? Does it hinder my ability to meet others as equals—and if yes, in what ways? Do I feel enabled, or even impelled, as a result of my status to enter the social order energetically? or do I feel isolated (whether in luxury or fear), or even immobilized?

The point is that economic status is the gateway between one's personal work and one's social work. It is a source of difficulty when, in comparing ourselves to others, we lose contact with either the goals of our own *or* society's *or* the universal well-being. When there is not an invigorating tension between those pulls, we have a work-related problem.

The counterpart of the discussion about "income" is a look at expenditure. A key term here is the "standard of living to which one aspires", a subtle term that brings together attitudes about identity with one's past and the existing social structure; about deserving and social justice; about awareness of personal, social and global resources; about the rhythm of life.

A good starting place is with recollection of childhood. Try recalling the physical environment of your home, writing or visualizing in detail its character. Were the furnishings inadequate, serviceable, substantial, or luxurious? Were there differences in quality in different parts of the house—why, do you suppose? Was there color and contrast, or quiet harmony, or makeshift ingenuity, or inattentiveness? On a scale from rigid orderliness to hopeless chaos, where did it fit in? Was it friendly and inviting, or just an okay place to be; was it a true home that fit your needs deeply, a prison that affronted your every sensibility, or something in between? What qualities have you preserved in your current home, and are these there from habit or from loving reconstruction? What qualities have you worked to get away from?

What about the necessities—food, shelter, clothes, attention to well-being? How were these provided...did the needs seem to be satisfied or did you feel deprived? If the latter, what was lacking—quantity, quality, concern for personal preferences? Did you compare what you had with others? If so, with what effect?

What was the family attitude about its status? Was there a feeling of mobility, or equilibrium? what mix was there of satisfaction, resignation, aspiration, desperation—overt or hidden? How did this mix affect you—did it permeate you, or did you rebel, or did you hold part of yourself aloof and in reserve?

Similar reflection is helpful in defining how you felt toward the neighbors' modes of life and (as you matured and became aware of a wider variety of living patterns) your changing attitude toward your native standard of living.

Finally, where are you now—are you comfortable with your standard of living? Have you experienced other ways of life and know which elements of your current style are essential and which are expendable? Do you have a sense of upper and lower limits you could accept without crisis?

What are you driven to change, and why—out of hunger for certain missing pieces? to acquire a different status and earn respect? to be able to organize your activities and committments more freely? to gain security and comfort for your family?

Reflections of this kind are an attempt to capture the subjective sense of our place in society. They can illuminate how close we have come, and how far we still need to go, in our search for social satisfaction.

They also reveal our relative ease or uneasiness with our status, and how much success we have had in our work. Someone whose standard of living has changed from being very unsatisfactory to being satisfactory has probably worked very hard at it, and very well. But, of course, "more satisfactory" doesn't necessarily mean more in quantity...someone can also work hard to achieve satisfaction with less.

On the other hand, someone whose standard of living has never been a problem, or who has fallen into comfort without effort, has either been given great good fortune and an extra responsibility somewhere else in life, or has a lot of remedial work ahead.

There are two other dimensions of the problem of "standard of living" to be considered here. One is the extent to which, in the course of our work, we have freed ourselves from the past and can formulate our goals in life freshly. The other is the effect of our inter-connection with other individuals in determining an appropriate way of life. The two are intertwined.

The life we are born into usually gives us two different kinds of starting place. One is a specific knowledge of what can, at least, sustain us; or, at best, nurture us deeply. This is a great gift—given bountifully to some, stingily to others, adequately to most. This early experience gives us basic knowledge of how to build comfort into our daily lives, and of where to find solace in times of need.

But all "things" pass—people die, houses are demolished or sold, customs become passé. So the gift contains tasks: to preserve the essentials and to recreate what we value when the original is gone. We must learn either how to "abstract" the value and find it in new, surprising ways, or to mourn its loss and learn to live creatively with its memory.

The other starting place is specific knowledge of what pains or disturbs us, what inhibits us in our instinctive search for satisfaction. This, I think, can be the more precious gift. Certainly smaller quantities of it seem needed, and only a few people appreciate it truly. For, as one reading of the tale of Sleeping Beauty has it, if the princess rejects the "wicked witch", she must sleep for several years: if we fail to accept pain as a gift of life—as a basis for understanding errors of judgment, bad habits, forces beyond our management—then we lapse into a dream world.

In contrast, I remember reading with awe the autobiography of Frederick Douglass, who escaped from slavery before the Civil War and became a great liberating spirit. Even as a very young boy he was able to take in the pain of his position—the physical cruelty, the psychological diminishment, the terrible restraints—yet retain clarity. He experienced his situation deeply, but he took the pain as a learning, not as punishment or mistake. He had the great strength of character to face the pain, trying to minimize or challenge it as appropriate but never denying it or taking it as a personal judgment.

Without having to rival Douglass' remarkable achievement, any of us can begin to see our early pain as the beginning of our lone journey in the world as a "particle of error". We can examine our childhood vulnerability, observe the methods we discovered for avoiding or denying or moving beyond the pain. We can see the "story" we devised about our lives, see how it has shaped our sense of expectation and possibility, see that it is not the only story that could be told.

The question here, as with the nice stuff, is how much work have we done? As we outgrew our initial vulnerability, have we gone back and confronted the pain anew so we can learn from it instead of just reacting to it? Have we grown beyond the conditioning of our early reflexes for survival, and become more curious about what was involved? Have we begun to think about the pain we inflict as well as that we endure? Can we see that either way, our involvement in pain is a call for change?

This thought returns us to the consideration of interdependence as we formulate our standard of living. Until now the discussion has focussed on subjective aspects, especially feelings about wants and needs. Pain, though, reflects the great objective Law of Reciprocity—about actions causing equal and opposite reactions, about "what goes around comes around", about give-and-take, about everything having a cost.

In an obvious way, no one determines his standard of living in a vacuum. It is formed in relation to others. To start with, my sense of what is important is greatly affected by those I live with. A household's well-being is dependent on how effectively each individual's wants and needs are sorted out, acknowledged, taken into account.

The success of each household is then up for comparison with the success of friends and neighbors. How much or little wealth do they have: how healthy do they seem? how stable or unstable, interesting or dull—such judgments may elicit envy, admiration, compassion, disdain.

Similarly neighborhoods, classes or groups of people, geographic regions, nations, or even continents in this age of communications, regard each other evaluatively. Our measures of luxury, poverty, well-being are changing, though; and initial judgments are often being replaced (healthily) by uncertainty. There is often a need to know more, to understand better what is involved in another's way of life. Are there hidden costs or benefits? Who receives, who gives? What do we have more than enough of that could be exchanged for what we have too little of? What is worth working for that our received social wisdom doesn't emphasize?

The information we use in this kind of evaluation is expanding. We still have the traditional puzzles of balancing immediate needs with long-range ones, of planning for what is now an insecure future both for ourselves and our growing children. But we are also forced to reflect on the lasting effects of our *means* of supporting a particular way of life. For instance, we find ourselves understanding that social disasters like unemployment, wide-spread disaffection and drug abuse, dreadful poverty even in lands of plenty, racism, war, chemical pollution are not accidents. They are outcomes of our social choices.

We begin also to realize, though perhaps dimly, that it does not suffice to find personal equilibrium within our native society. Once it may have seemed enough to mature, to find one's place, to succeed in a job and raise a family. Now—as it appears that *we* bring on the catastrophes which threaten what we work for—inner logic compels us to question "what we have always done."

So we are faced with a challenge. In a way parallel to our search (cf. Chapter 2) for a meaning of home and family that is less literal, less conventional than our language is accustomed to conveying, we need to re-interpret "standard of living."

I suspect the change requires a much clearer understanding of reciprocity. The means of life are given and we are obligated to pass them on. Luxury is for a moment, not the norm. (Parenthetically, while admiring beautiful estates, the thought arose, "How nice that they exist, but how unfair that they should be owned. What if they were made available on rotation to a lot of people?") There is no such thing as a permanent status quo: I am not guaranteed anything more than the adventure of living.

This thinking rests on an intuition of the flux, the kaleidoscopic re-arrangements life involves us in. I remember seeing an exhibit of water-color pictures depicting scenes at the beach. The artist showed dozens of people in the ocean. Some were thrown over by the waves. Some were riding them tentatively. Some were plunging in. And many more were on the shore watching. I ask myself, how do I fare in the sea of life? how do I relate to the people, objects, the flux around me?

Lurking in the cellar during the above discussion is my personal conviction that social conventions cannot adequately guide our individual lives. This understanding has evolved slowly, often accompanied by anxiety. Who am I to challenge what is generally accepted around me? What will happen if I say that the Emperor has no clothes?

My experience has yielded two phases of response to these questions: First, a testing process, and second, "taking a stand."

The first phase is the time during which we define our beliefs, allow received wisdom to jostle against intuition and experience. The anxiety I spoke of may result in silence, a failure to voice one's perceptions and feelings. It may equally, though, manifest itself as rebellion—a difficulty in taking in others' beliefs or thoughts, an insistence that "I am right" rather than that "I am I." Rebelliousness can include a resistance to admitting possible error, to being shown that my formulation of a situation may be shallow, or over-stated, or over-simplified, or factually incorrect.

At stake here is a willingness to work continuously toward a formulation that is true to ourselves, yet open to change as more information becomes available. We can accept being in error without giving up our right to make independent determinations, be heard, and be taken into account. Yet also we need to be clear that another's formulation that does not take my condition—my being—into account is inadequate, incomplete.

After a period of testing, as a sense of moral certitude is approached, we can seek to express ourselves and stand up "politically" for what we believe. This is a kind of work that is too often praised only in the abstract, or in retrospect, as in the eulogies given the Martin Luther Kings of our world ten years after their death, by the very people who reviled them alive. "Political work" in progress is done without guidelines, with no duplicable models. It has its inevitable mistakes and shortcomings mercilessly exposed. To move into creative political activity (of however limited a venue) with the intention of engaging one's beliefs seriously—not just for the sake of "winning" or attaining power—is perhaps the most demanding *work* of all.

The ability to engage in "moral action" on behalf of our tested values, while still maintaining our activities within (and our respect for) the on-going social flow, is the fullest measure I can see of success as a social being.

Part III: Self and Other

I have an identity: it's what I answer to the question, "Who are you?"
It constitutes aspects of being that have been named, acknowledged and
remembered.

My being, though, is indisputably more encompassing than my
identity. It includes, also, everything I do but don't count or don't accept,
i.e. that I don't identify with; everything that I don't know how to name or
characterize clearly, i.e. that I can't identify.

There are words used to point to these aspects of self that we can't talk
about readily, words like "unconscious", "psyche", "inner self", "soul".
But these words indicate rather than describe, and alone are not very
revealing.

So what can be made of this "other self" and the world it exists in? To
begin with, we know it is operable in our lives. Others see us in
unexpected ways, to various effect. Someone notices my coloration and is
attracted to me because of it. A salesman sees a streak of vanity I'm
unaware of and plays on it to sell me an expensive suit.

Even alone, I may find myself at cross-purposes. I want to get
married, but the relationships I choose to enter never work out. I know
I'm capable of magnificent deeds, yet I'm frustrated in my efforts to

succeed. I have a conviction that despite my current miseries there is another life where the "true me" will shine. I have dreams at night that seem more real than my waking hours. I keep meeting people who, as if by magic, lead me into new adventures, or who make me question the very foundations of my life.

All these are examples of a dialogue being created between the revealed and the concealed self. Life can be like an improvised theater scene. It sometimes seems designed to dramatize—to bring into a form that has significance and impact—the relationship between our known selves and the previously unrealized. Can these seemingly random experiences cohere into a way of understanding? Can we integrate "the other" with the life we know?

In contemporary society, there seem to be four salient, purposeful approaches to the "other" side of identity—spirituality, psychology, philosophy, and mysticism. Many practices and studies exist which overlap two or three of these approaches, but it is worth looking at them each separately.

First, though, I will examine a special case, which is probably the most common path to "the other," a way that often seems chosen for, rather than by, us. This is the path followed in the name of love and sexuality.

Seven

Love and Sex (as a spiritual discipline)

Over the centuries, great leaders and thinkers have understood that a crucial part of life was finding a correct estimation of ego. It cannot be demeaned, as that leaves us subject to others' tyranny. But if it is magnified, we ourselves become tyrants.

Most of us have a "self" that is splintered, with some parts in balance, some parts crushed and some inflated. For the disproportioned parts, a spiritual discipline is called for, a set of practices with two goals. First, to reduce the greed, power-hunger, defensiveness and general selfishness of the "me-above-all" part of human personhood. Second, to instill faith in our doubting selves that we may act as agents of creative power.

Such disciplines have often been carried out in a religious context. People have sought to diminish their boundless desires (or the perplexity resulting from these desires) by practices like prayer, self-denial, obedience to a doctrine and order, submission to a spiritual master. Accommodation to a life of hardship has often been accomplished by coming to accept circumstances as God's will.

Practices of this kind are still undertaken by millions. Large numbers of other people involve themselves with similar but non-religious practices such as those spawned from the great twentieth century discipline of psychotherapy. (Both of these approaches will be examined in the next chapter.) But the number of Americans who submit intentionally to the on-going, radical self-examination implicit in any of these disciplines is manifestly small.

This situation may mirror the loosening grip of oppressive material circumstance in our society. As the extremes of deprivation have been reduced, and some civic buffers have been established against overbearing governmental power, few people seem driven to find an authority to help them explain, justify or transcend their material conditions by diminishing personal desire.

Instead the rights to *want*, to *claim*, to *possess*, to *enjoy* have been raised to ranking principles of conduct. The popular focus has shifted from ego-reduction to ego-support—to discovering why I think so little of myself that I don't demand more from life.

Self-affirmation is a legitimate quest. Sholem Aleichem wrote a story about a poverty-stricken, down-trodden peasant of the old Jewish Pale in eastern Europe. This peasant, Bontshe Schweig, went through life suffering every kind of deprivation and degradation, never raising his voice in protest or prayer, humbly accepting his lot. So when he died, he was carried straight to heaven as only the holiest of saints are. And at the gates of Paradise, where his admission could be challenged, even the Devil's advocate did not protest.

A troop of angels bore him into Paradise, and to the the throne of the Almighty himself, who spoke to Bontshe saying, "No inhabitant of earth has suffered so terribly while demanding so little of life. Now as your reward you can have whatever you want"

Bontshe looked blank, dazed by the splendor, unable to summon courage to speak. Finally, eyes still fixed on the ground, he stuttered out his request. "Please, may I have a crust of bread." And the angels wept.

No, a human soul is not so pallid and meagre. Yes, we often need help in affirming our immense capacities, our native desire to use and satisfy them. But we also need to understand what our individual limits are, what goals and forms of action are proper, how our powers relate to the other forces of the universe. We still have to "adjust to reality." And this kind of knowledge has to be attained—or rather deciphered—from a confusion of signs, symbols, impulses, directives, manifestoes, persuasions, seductions that fill our minds from inside and out.

It would seem natural to look for guidance through this maze, to seek discipleship. But in an age when authority has become suspect (especially for young people) and when all traditions are known to be inadequate (although many can be immensely helpful), more and more we have given ourselves over to "experience" to teach us. And frequently the first testing ground of our power, and our limits, is the field of sexuality.

This means of entering spiritual discipleship is, of course, not new. For although the ancient Greeks made the distinction between Agape (spiritual love) and Eros (sexual love) with some merit, there is also precedent and good cause for our use of the one word Love as common ground.

We can look at Christ's parables which suggest that worldly love is only a literal, less perfect version of Christian love. We can look at Chaucer's unbridled Wife of Bath who, battling her way through numerous sexual adventures, finally recognizes a true mate whom she can love altruistically. The plaints and poems of the Renaissance courtly lovers—full of ambivalent devotion to mortal gods and goddesses—still echo in our popular music and literature (not to mention in letters to Dear Abby.) D.H. Lawrence, in his story "The Man Who Died", wrote of a Jesus who learns to love with his body as well as his spirit, who in the heat of coupling with the Goddess Isis exclaims, "I am risen." Our culture is replete with examples showing the sexual and spiritual to have a vital, if elusive, connection. Moreover, where once Romeo and Juliet were looked on as courageous rebels in their pursuit of romance, Americans now grow up expecting, even searching for, love and passion, though without any idea of the turbulence this pursuit will cast them into.

For however primed by our culture to look for salvation in romance and sex, we are not prepared for what is to come. We are educated to have unbounded expectations...then the bonds of love come as something of a shock. We fall in love or lust, stirred by an unexamined, inexplicable passion which defies resolution. "Something" is wanted desperately; and in trying to find what it is, in trying to attain the goals as they have been misrepresented, our identified selves (i.e. our egos) are put through ordeal after ordeal.

It is amazing. We find ourselves doing what we could never have imagined doing, thinking and feeling in new ways altogether. We are uplifted, we are dashed to the ground. One minute we swear we will do anything for the beloved, the next we are ready to kill him or her. We are mute, unable to ask for the Unspeakable; then bold and commanding. We desire just one night of passion; we vow to be united forever. We want total freedom, while in jealousy we deny our lovers all freedom.

Suddenly our expectations and ideas are shaken apart. We are toe-to-toe in combat with the mighty Other, and our very sanity is at stake. Such is the stuff of spiritual suffering, such is the form it most commonly takes in this country...and increasingly so, as young people are denied access to most other adult pursuits or responsibilities that can test their limits.

In this light, it should not be surprising that most traditional societies have kept close rein on sexual partnering. Life-mates are selected pragmatically and/or by customary means, often by others. Erotic fantasy and sensuality are limited: perhaps condoned only in youth, or only with a certain class of women. Sexuality may be justified only for reproduction, or only within the bounds of legal or religious sanction.

The gradual erosion of traditional authority in matters of personal life, and the simultaneous growth of leisure and choice, have together brought love into a peculiar prominence. In fact, it has every appearance of being the most common form of spiritual discipline in our times.

Compared to disciplines entered into by calling or sober choice, compared to disciplines organized according to long-established practices or unifying authority, Love is a uniquely democratic, chaotic spiritual path. After all, both partners in the process are likely to be untrained and ill-prepared for the "curriculum" they have entered into. The goals are unclear, the roles undefined; the constraints—ethical, social, practical—have become increasingly debatable.

This chapter speculates on how love and sex can be experienced as a spiritual discipline instead of a haphazard trial to be endured. There are several elements in the pursuit of love that may, in the abstract, seem irreconcilable. But just as in a physical exercise where, for instance, you are instructed to twist the torso to one side yet keep the hips facing forward, apparent contradiction can be resolved into an instructive action.

To begin, let us look at the components of attraction and mating, and the paradox that arises when one of the most deep-rooted, instinctual parts of life is subject to intense social influence.

It is a fact, borne out by psychological research but unexplained, that early in childhood each individual identifies a group of qualities he or she is attracted to in a special, exciting way. For most people, this group of qualities—colors, fragrances, shapes, movements—remains relatively constant, a core of impulsive erotic interest that we have little control over. Most of us, for most of our lives, are triggered sexually by the presence of these qualities.

There is also a second aspect of sexuality involving the need for physical affirmation and release from tension. We need the freedom to make contact, to touch and be touched, to express our impulses and have them received: to achieve intercourse. However, we don't necessarily attain this contact with those we are erotically drawn to. There is an intricate calculus at work in determining where, when and with whom such sexual release is possible and appropriate. One factor is social training. We are instructed early in life as to who are desirable partners, and we observe: who in our circle is in fact admired and who disparaged? which partnerships are praised, which tolerated, which ridiculed? What was seen as proper for the giving and taking of affection in the home environment? in friends' homes? in the media?

Another factor is the force of circumstance—being placed in a situation where intense need and unusual opportunity bring about unexpected, often temporary, partnering. These unions may, though, have long-term effects ranging from producing a child to passing beyond social taboo, to inducing life-long guilt.

Another element at play is intimacy, that is discovering with another a mutual sensitivity to the special private life that each of us cherishes within. A deep kinship, a commonality and receptivity can be formed with unexpected people. The range of partners in these special interchanges (which, to me, are undeniably sexual) seem to be limited only by our psychological preparedness to give or accept such intimacy. I have felt such a bond with old people and children, with clients and colleagues, with people of both genders, even with natural beings—animals, trees, the sun, the beach.

Our readiness to act on the flowing sexual impulses from any of these sources may be restricted by any of a number of things: social approval; ethical issues of responsibility; practical constraints of time, privacy and consequences; moral or religious convictions; contradictory obligations. But when we choose not to act on them, for any of these reasons, we need not deny the feelings themselves...nor the knowledge that we are not so different from those who *do* act when we do not.

Intimacy, this giving and receiving of innermost trust, is perhaps the most voluntary form of sexual attraction. It may also be a central factor in finding a long-term mate, and is certainly the clearest link between Eros and Agape, sexual love and spiritual love.

Sexual attraction also has a romantic and imaginative component which can be understood as a search for unity and completion of one's self, a longing for harmony, beauty, liberation. This element frequently includes an attraction of opposites: dark and fair, powerful and petite, active and contemplative. But romantic inspiration also comes from subtler kinds of admiration, be they physical, psychological, intellectual, aesthetic or spiritual.

One issue here is gender, the urge for mating between what are conceived as "masculine" and "feminine" aspects. We tend to reduce this to considerations of male and female, but the issue is more complicated. Even at the most basic physiological level there are borderline cases where it is difficult to assign gender to individuals. There are hermaphrodites with the sexual organs of both genders, and transsexuals who deny their physical attributes and take on the opposite gender identity.

But even the vast majority of us who have a physically-determined gender identity are in for some confusion. We all go through a process of gender-modeling, comparing ourselves to ideals of our gender in both internal and external ways.

Externally, we check our bodies and demeanor. Am I muscular enough to be a real man, or are my breasts becoming large enough to qualify me as a woman? Am I admired for my feminine charm and ability to attract flattering attention, or for my masculine aggressiveness and daring?

In this process, romantic admiration is often felt for members of the same gender who have the culturally indicated traits *par excellence*. Perhaps these idols serve as a pre-image of one's future developed personage, or perhaps win admiration for what one feels expected (but seems unlikely) to attain. Sometimes, the "unperfected" trait is sought in group bonding with others of the same gender—as if many of us together muster up sufficiently the quality we are supposed to have individually.

Furthermore, each person has an internal self-image that may not correspond with physique. A frail-looking woman can feel herself as quite prepossessing; a giant of a man can feel powerless. How can these contradictions be maintained?

Also many of us have, in the language of Gestalt Therapy, psychological "holes" in our physical awareness. For example, an acquaintance told me he used to feel that he had no chest until he put on the jacket of someone he was drawn to and, magically, sensation suddenly flowed into his torso. In a case like that, a romantic longing may incline toward anyone who seems able to fill the gap.

So in several ways romantic feelings can lead to surprising relationships, with people outside our conventional expectations of a proper mate. These relationships may or may not be enduring...but they must be endured. Often they are entered into with guilt, fear, denial, self-abnegation. In other words, we are usually terribly off-balance in entering a romantic liaison. We "fall" in love.

In this state, we may well disregard temporarily all our other values; and here is a source of difficulty. Only when romance is combined with caring, respect and honesty; only when times of "falling" are matched with times of balance, can Eros and Agape come together fittingly. Shakespeare's comic heroines are wonderful examples of head-first longing modulated with prudence. But a song by the Eagles also says it well: "I got a peaceful, easy feeling/ and I know you won't let me down/ 'cause I'm already standing on the ground."

There is another destabilizing element in sexual attraction: power relations. Part of the sexual "hunt" involves searching out partners with whom we can feel ourselves as masters able to extend fully our strength; or, conversely, it might be to seek a situation where we can allow ourselves briefly to give up life's perpetual striving instead to yield to an outside will. These needs can be part of a flexible, changing relationship; or they might be isolated and fixed in a roleplaying enacted with different partners at different times.

A related issue is pain. Clinical researchers report that the brain activity does not seem different in registering pain or extreme pleasure. Sexual activity is often a play at the border of pain and pleasure, and one of the heights of sexual experience is being carried on waves of passion beyond everyday boundaries and cautions, into areas of physical and emotional abandon.

Often, however, we are so constricted by habit and self-image that we are not able to enter this liberating process consciously or willingly. We may depend on fantasy to create a scene that induces experimentation. Or we may adopt a more rigid kind of role-playing, turning intimacy into psycho-drama.

These cases may seem bizarre to those on the outside; but externals do not tell the story. People may be involved in the posturing of singles bars, or the elaborate play of submission/dominance, in seductive costumery, or cross-gender dressing. In any of these situation, spontaneous and considerate—even caring—relating is as possible as in the more familiar, socially-approved models of romantic coupling.

For the essence is always in the *quality of the relating*. Responsiveness to the partner, frankness and vulnerability, intelligence and humor and freedom: these, not "proper form", are what allows sexuality to become a kind of loving. After all, no one "has" an orgasm: rather, the orgasm has us...and the more fully we are moved to share that potent, awesome experience with another, the more we are moved by and opened to the great force of Love. This is how sexuality leads to knowledge of the Universe's creative powers. With this in mind, we can ask what each of us has made of our own loving and erotic experiences.

> To start, have I ever fallen in love? If so, where did the experience leave me—did I learn from it about myself and my place in life? was I more enriched by contact with the other, or more diminished, or about equally affected? Were we able to establish an equable relationship, or were we always embroiled in passion?

> Was I sufficiently changed by the experience that I moved on to other kinds of relationships, or have I tended to repeat the same pattern with other, similar people? If the latter, what is it that I am addicted to, why do I seek these qualities in a situation that tends toward failure and disappointment—how do I sabotage the relationship to prevent it from being beneficial?

Have I allowed myself to recognize love for more than one kind of person? Have I been drawn to (without necessarily becoming sexually engaged with) people of different kinds of coloration and build, with diverse character traits or temperaments? Have I been involved both as The Lover and The Beloved—very different experiences; and if not, is it because of indifference, or lack of occasion? or is there a fear that could be fruitfully explored?

It is, of course, also possible to love without feeling strong erotic attraction i.e. to feel compassion for, or share piquant intimacy with, another or others. What Eros and Agape have in common is the blurring of the self's boundaries; and a self-effacing union without sensuality has equal claim to being called "intercourse" as does genital contact. With so-called Platonic relationships, the range of those we can love is bounded only by obedience to social convention, caution and habit. So it is worth considering the extent that we have let curiosity and open-mindedness lead us into the world. Have we given ourselves lovingly to people of widely differing ages? Have we revealed our inner selves to both men and women?

At this point, it becomes crucial to look more closely at gender roles. With few exceptions, most of us have a clear notion of gender identity (being male or female) but gender role is much more uncertain, as it is primarily determined by culture rather than biology.

Within a society there are specified activities, duties, privileges accorded solely to each gender; and there are certain manners of dress and behavior deemed appropriate for each. Typically there are also strongly suggested patterns for how the genders should interact—in which situations each gender is assigned dominance or deference, when equality is to be tolerated.

The problems here begin as individuals realize they do not fall neatly into the models fashioned by their culture. On one hand, a person may have physical characteristics or in-born tendencies or idiosyncratic preferences or family-derived habits that run counter to cultural conformity.

On the other hand, in a rapidly changing world where knowledge of other cultures has become readily available, the authority of "tradition" has been radically weakened. There is less and less assurance about what a man or woman "should" be like at a given time and place. Looking across time and cultures, in fact, there seem to be very few consistent defining features of masculinity and femininity—especially now that technology has reduced the areas where men's typical (though much over-stated) superiority of strength and endurance is called on, and that work practices call women equally into the labor force. The innate differences between the genders become harder to locate outside the physical roles involved in reproduction and child nurturance.

Still we sense a genuine difference, and there is a strong inner call for men to know themselves as men among men, for women to seek solidarity with other women. We continue to differentiate our behavior toward members of each gender in important ways. Clearly this is one of the most basic aspects of every culture's socialization, about as primary as teaching control of physiological and emotional impulses. To be isolated from our identified gender group, to feel the threat of ostracism, is extraordinarily unnerving for most of us. So the confusion about gender roles strikingly present in our culture is creating deep anxiety. Is it now acceptable for women freely to cultivate their non-domestic abilities and ambitions, seek to define themselves independently of men and family? Is it acceptable for men to express their aesthetic or contemplative sides, to reveal their insecurities and areas of ineffectiveness, to show affection and admiration (even for each other) openly? Yes? No? Sometimes?

New definitions of gender may be a-borning; but the social need for definitions seems always to be present. For this reason, crossing the gender-role barrier is one of the great challenges of the sexual way to spiritual liberation. Unless we are able to pass beyond those pre-determined images of who we need to prove ourselves against sexually, and how we are supposed to perform in the doing, we will find ourselves going in circles rather than journeying onward.

Finally, this discussion requires us to look at how love and sexuality relate to our society's moral order. In question here is the ability to incorporate love and sexuality into relationships that serve as a basis for creative social living. Most frequently the network of relationships built around intimacy, recreation, passion and (pro) creation is called a family. What has been called the "nuclear family" of mother, father and children, however, derives not from a universal standard. It springs from our specific social history, with its particular set of socio-economic pressures and its particular notions of appropriate sexual expression. As social demands have begun to change, and as additional modes of sexual expression have become more or less legitimized, the meaning of "family" has likewise come into question.

"Marriage", i.e. the enduring relationship between two people at the center of a family, still seems to be the most usual basis of social living. Yet marriage, too, has been considerably freed in form. It can be religious, civil, common-law. It now unscandalously (if relatively infrequently) crosses class, religious, ethnic and national boundaries. It sometimes includes long-lasting homosexual unions. And it is more commonly viewed as experimental rather than eternal—a change that has come, perhaps, simply because our lives are longer and more varied than before. Or perhaps because of a collective loss of faith. Or because of an acceptance of changes. Or from a widespread unwillingness to work through hardship. Or all the above.

There is even some small recognition that people can be involved in fairly stable families that do not have marriage at their center: single parents with children; small domestic communities; people deeply involved in religious or social institutions. In all such cases, though, there is no identified sexual partner, and this means that sexuality is either cut away from its social moorings or has to be worked with very carefully.

Of course even people in marriage-type relationships have to deal with aspects of their sexuality that are not readily expressed with, or satisfied by, the given partner. Married folk are not exempt from using fantasy (with or without masturbation). Who among us has not at least imagined flirtation, anonymous sex, or affairs of various sorts? Who does not have some odd notion that seems too crazy to share with the particular person we are wed to? Who has not just wanted to be sexual at a time inopportune for the partner?

Domestic partnerships are often entered into without adequate knowledge of, or regard for, *both people's* sexual depths. Growing intimacy, sometimes aided by counselling, may allow sexuality to remain alive and creative...but not necessarily. If deep-seated elements of sexuality are unattended to, or if sexual feelings stimulated by other contacts cannot somehow be brought home, sexual interest may become either suffocated or extra-marital.

On the other side of the fence are those for whom sex is not at all a family affair. It is an adventure of experimentation and discovery, a recreational sport, or even a tortuous psychological necessity.

Sexuality of these kinds is frequently perceived of as a threat to domesticated sexuality, and is often condemned or suppressed. In fact, it may stimulate untried fantasies and hidden impulses in those whose sex lives are contained within a domestic ideal. Indeed unconstrained sexuality *is* threatening, and each culture has taboo lines that demarcate what has been deemed as dangerous to familial sexuality. The Forbidden is labelled, transgressions are punished.

Each of us plays out our sexuality against socially prescribed boundaries, finding ways to come to terms with "sexual outlaws" and also with our own outlaw tendencies. Societies are correct in estimating the destabilizing potential of sexuality, and justified in teaching protective guidelines for young people as they move beyond self-defined eroticism into sexual relationship.

However, many societies (preeminently our own) err in the violence of their judgments and reactions toward what is deemed sexual deviance.

For sexuality is a multi-faceted, even cunning, aspect of humanhood that contains in hidden form great spiritual intelligence. To foreclose too soon on our possibilities can be stultifying; to cut ourselves off from others who have followed unconventional routes of exploring sexuality is to deprive ourselves of crucial intelligence.

Rather than trying to "control" sexuality, we can consider ourselves as sexual beings in constant movement toward fertilizing interpenetration with our surroundings. We may at different times be moved passionately, tentatively, intuitively, even rationally: the trick is to turn our sexual impulses into creative, productive relationship.

There is no doubt that the Path of Love is a valid and powerful path toward spiritual understanding. Yet it may also be a treacherous path and, in our times when it is the most accessible and natural path for many, we would do well to accord it its due. Ann Landers and Human Sexuality classes are commendable; but most people need more guidance than those resources offer...and less interference than social dictates are wont to impose.

Eight

Spirituality & Psychology:

encounters with the Other

Spirituality begins with a belief: what we know as ourselves and our lives is not to be taken at face value. Mortal life is, perhaps, a piece in a giant puzzle beyond man's comprehension; or a pale reflection of a dazzling reality. It may be considered as the handiwork of an infallible creator; or an an unfinished experiment trying to complete itself. It may be seen as nothing but a play of the mind, insubstantial of itself, disguising a hard-to-comprehend Reality. It may be conceived of as a distorted or despoiled image of the Creator, needing purification of heart and mind to be perceived rightly; or as an alienated fragment of creation needing to find its way home. It may even be examined as the locus of a terrible struggle between Good and Evil that we are only vaguely aware of.

In whatever way this known self—our visible life—is imagined, its spiritual significance springs primarily in its relation to a creative, purposeful process, or a Supreme Entity, whose superiority calls forth allegiance and duteous behavior. In other words, according to the spiritual perspective, the known self will live in error, frustration or sin unless it learns to harmonize itself with the greater Other. Moreover, in this way of looking, the true adventure of life lies in the process of learning how to act in wholeness: the spiritual intent is a more perfect union of known self and Other.

Spiritual belief, then, implies that life has purpose or direction, can be improved, and has principles of behavior to be accorded to toward those ends. Belief is a source of hope in overcoming feelings of impotence, futility, aimlessness. It provides inspiration to counter disappointment or despair. It instills a need for continual learning and understanding in the process of discovering how to live rightly.

Belief also implies that the individual human is incomplete and insufficient, with limited knowledge and judgment. The nature of the Great Being can be experienced; but as that experience is translated to human terms—is interpreted by human minds—it falls subject to error. In spiritual terms, life is an experiment that continues until one's humanity (including one's individuality and mortality) is transcended.

Out of this perspective come several elements common to most modern religions. A vision of the Great Being. A story depicting the creation of the natural universe, including a characterization of the human individual and its relations to the creative force, to other individuals and to nature. A version of time and history. A proposal for escaping the bondage of time, suffering and death by attaining a correct relationship to the Great Being and the other beings of the universe.

Religions are often based on the super-human understanding, or life example, of chosen individuals who have fully encountered the Other, and of their immediate disciples. From their words and deeds are derived principles of right living that are meant to guide lesser individuals to a better, more satisfying life; to a more compassionate relationship with others; to a stronger, more fruitful connection with the Other.

It is important to recognize that spirituality can exist outside particular religious traditions. An individual with spiritual instincts can approach the tasks of spirituality without adhering to any particular doctrine, or with guidance from many. On the other hand, while spiritual experience lies at the foundation of all religions, religions tend to become social institutions as well as spiritual vehicles when they attempt to order the lives of a group of followers.

As institutions, religions tend to become conservative, controlled by vested interests and often guided by tenth-hand interpretations of the words of the early founders rather than by fresh revelation. Moreover, they tend to respond slowly if at all to new knowledge and changing social situations.

To their credit, organized religions provide mass instruction of basic spiritual wisdom, a kind of spiritual elementary school. They also provide support systems for facing crisis, giving both tangible and intangible evidence that an individual is not alone but lives as part of a larger social entity. Organized religions also often instill confidence in their members' worth, and their ability to find peace of mind even in the face of hardship and crisis. Yet sometimes the social effectiveness of an organized religion comes at cost to its spiritual roots. Here are some questions to consider:

— Does the church under consideration teach *about* spirituality rather than helping to create spiritual experience or insight?

— Does it inspire self-confidence at the expense of others, raising its adherents up only by putting others down? Does it champion the well-being of its supporters as a higher good than the well-being of the commonweal?

— Does it claim to have answers, rather than questions; knowledge rather than wisdom? Does it have contempt for non-believers rather than curiosity about and interest in them? Does it prefer obedience to investigation, conformity to individuality?

— Does it break into antagonistic factions and sects rather than reformulate itself to accommodate difference? Does it claim to be The Way, rather than *a* way to help people look for The Way? Does it attack others for their differing beliefs rather than just presenting its own beliefs as persuasively as possible? Does it provoke self-righteous belligerence in its own defense rather than compassionate action on behalf of others?

The former choices are the methods of organizational and social politicking, the latter the way of spirituality. The former emphasize belonging, security, reassurance; the latter are an attempt to use the inspiration of the past to discover new ways of relating to the Other. The former may have a useful social function, but the latter is spirituality in action.

The other currently legitimized approach to direct encounter with the Other is the 20th century's unique contribution—psychology. Unfortunately, though, the term "psychology" has lost its primary meaning through inappropriate usage. Contrary to school catalogues and textbook titles, those branches of study which seek ways to analyze and manipulate the reflex activities of the human animal are not psychology, and would more accurately be called behavioral technology.

The root meaning of the word comes from the Greek "psyche" meaning soul, so psychology is the study of the soul. The endeavor of that study is not to change or motivate or improve. Rather, it is to seek knowledge of the unknown with all the faculties and skills of the known; to arrange encounters between Known and Other, seeking to turn those encounters into a fuller understanding of reality.

This is not the place for a brief history of psychological practice. It is, though, to the point to look into some of the major approaches to encountering the psyche that twentieth century psychology has made available to us.

Sigmund Freud was the man who initiated the contemporary systematic study of how the Other manifests itself in each person's daily life. His theory about the Unconscious called attention to the fact that the Other contains not just more of the things we desire—power, wisdom, compassion, etc.—but also qualities we reject. These latter are qualities lacking in our make-up naturally or perhaps after early experience led us to believe them to be dangerous, inappropriate, unsuccessful or frightening. (Typically, these traits include hatred, greed, envy, fear, lust, and the like.)

Our personalities develop to make use of the effective, approved qualities at our command, and these make up our identity. The rejected parts exist nonetheless, and seek expression. This aspect of the Other seems like the great opponent rather than the great sustainer and in Hebrew, the original language of the Bible, the word for opponent, or hinderer, is Satan. So Freud's first great teaching was, in one respect, that the devil must get his due.

The motives or desires we have denied ("repressed") can be found at work whenever our imperious wills let down their defenses, in everything we do not consciously choose. Freud studied closely such phenomena as small accidents of speech or behavior (so-called "Freudian slips"); coincidental resemblances of people and objects in one's current life to recollections of the past, especially from early childhood; and, perhaps most prominently, dreams.

Freud also contributed the notion of "free association". He suggested that when we express freely whatever passes through us at a given time (without trying to formulate or censor the material to make it appropriate or acceptable) the unconscious will reveal itself. Artists of all kinds, as well as those concerned with therapy (healing), have used this insight to great advantage—welcoming and learning from what comes forth rather than attempting to push it down or conceal it if it is unseemly.

C.G. Jung, one of Freud's students and early collaborators, broadened and deepened the conception of what the psyche is.

From his studies, clinical observations and personal experiences, he came to believe that the individual psyche is rooted below the individual's birth- and family-history. The kinds of associations and dream-images Freud noted as relating back to early childhood, Jung believed to come from a "collective unconscious", a shared pool of significant images, ideas, stories that shaped the contents of the human mind. These significant forms he called "archetypes."

Freud's search to meet the Other focussed on uncovering memories of actual experience in the individual's life, discovering what had been repressed. Jung, instead, drew up a kind of chart of human nature and said, in effect, that whichever of the qualities listed on the chart are not evident in a particular individual's behavior must be present in that person's unconscious—in the person's "shadow", as he termed it.

Moreover, Jung wrote, we exist in a collective process. This means, on one hand, that we work out our encounters with the Shadow in collaboration with others. As Freud postulated that an individual's "slips" were not accidents but indicators of an inner dialogue; so Jung postulated that interpersonal encounters were not coincidental but were the result of both people's unconscious working mutually. Further, the action of communities, or even nations, were similarly being "arranged" by the encounter of the collective consciousness (recorded history) with the collective unconscious. This process Jung called "synchronicity."

If Jung's perspective is taken, then psychology becomes another enterprise in trying to comprehend the Great Being. It differs from the spiritual enterprise in several respects, however. First, it does not presuppose an original source of being nor a purpose in existence.

Second, it is "non-normative": it does not speak about right or wrong, or about achieving some ideal state of being. Instead it aims at knowing without fear what is going on—what "stories" we're living in, what archetypal forces are at work around and through us.

It also aims at recognizing and recovering the elements lost in the Shadow (especially unfamiliar ways of perceiving experience and functioning in life) and of "integrating" these uncovered elements with our known selves. (This process requires giving up the rule of our developed skills. It calls for limiting our personal success as specialists in order to engage life with fuller awareness...more ecologically so to speak. For example, if I am accustomed to trusting and acting primarily on my intuition, I need to discover my senses and my reason and my emotions.)

A third goal of Jungian psychology is "individuation". This process has two aspects. One is attaining an understanding of the unique combination of qualities and perspectives each one of us has as an individual. After all, no one else experiences life just as I do, and there are certain actions that no one else sees as necessary or possible, that no one else is in a position to carry out. The second aspect is that, if we then take on the task of making our individuality effective, we are led beyond the conventions of our social education into other realms of consciousness and experience. We explore what lies beyond the given boundaries more or less fully, and our lives are transformed in varying degrees each time we move beyond group norms, beyond the customs and habits, ideas and beliefs that compose our known personality. As we direct attention into these uncharted waters, we enter into the true subject matter of psychology.

Two additional psychological approaches to the Other deserve mention here for their impact on contemporary thinking. One is the analysis by Wilhelm Reich (another of Freud's early circle) of "body armoring." He concluded that the way we hold our bodies, how we breathe and move and use our sensing faculties are all restricted by defensive responses such as to fear, cultural training and trauma. All physical disciplines—from Yoga to ballet, from practicing a sport to studying mime, from bodybuilding to one of the numerous body therapies derived from Reich's own work—take us beyond the customary use of our bodies. In so doing, they have a therapeutic potential: the effects of changes occurring can be explored from a psychological perspective.

The other approach (exemplified in the model of Gestalt Therapy formulated by Fritz Perls) is based on the understanding that what we experience in the "outside world" is in crucial ways a "projection" of ourselves. In other words, our experience is typically shaped and colored by the categories and qualities we recognize or repress in ourselves, rather than by fresh, unbiased observation. Thus, often we are not experiencing the Other, but are in effect talking to and about ourselves even though we seem to be addressing something or someone else. For example, I may mistrust someone for what I know is untrustworthy in myself rather than for any threat genuinely evidenced by the other.

The close study of individual experience by means of any of these or related approaches constitutes the clinical practice of psychology. Often this discipline is carried out in a context called psychotherapy.

"Therapy" and psychological counselling have become increasingly common treatments for a variety of human ills and crises. Pointed research and intuitive observation have been collected over several decades, and there is a quantity of information about how people communicate and mis-communicate; how we trigger each others' fears and defenses; how unproductive "systems" develop in mutual or communal avoidance of a problem. There is also a lot known about the onset and working-through of personality problems and blockages to maturation.

Counselors and therapists thus can often help people move out of situations they seem stuck in, or are scared to enter. This kind of intervention should be viewed, however, as applied psychology or psychological first-aid, rather than as psychology itself. These efforts are honorable, worthwhile and often effective; but they are not truly a study of the psyche.

On the other hand, psychological practitioners also may function as spiritual teachers. Psychotherapy of this kind (which may be differentiated from counselling) is usually entered into as a lengthy learning process with no short-term goals. In this case, the role of the therapist is not specifically to ease pain or help solve problems, but to lead the client to perceptions of how he or she frames experience—what emphases or interpretations are adopted by reflex, what information is omitted by purposeful if unconscious blindness, etc.

Therapy of this kind is a very tricky affair. The client is most often not sure why he or she has begun nor how to proceed...and is usually in a state of extreme insecurity. Moreover, the therapist is not perceived clearly at all: hopes, fears, doubts, needs from the past as well as the present are projected onto the therapist as a figure of authority and power.

The process of discovering what the therapist actually offers —of determining if this is a worthwhile relationship and of determining how best to make use of it—is perhaps the most difficult part of therapy.

In judging the progress of therapy and the relationship with the therapist, there are a few questions I've found useful:

Are you able to establish a way of communicating experience that gives the therapist the kind of material she or he wants and gives you a feeling of discovery or unburdening in the process?

Are you able to speak about your feelings toward the therapist and raise doubts about the process...and be given a response that informs your choice to continue or not?

Are you becoming freer to bring to the therapist sensitive and anxiety-producing material that you don't reveal to others?

Are you at least sometimes eager for your meetings, and also sometimes in dread of them?

Do you happen onto surprising ideas and recollections during your times together?

Do you begin to understand what the therapist looks for, how she or he thinks and responds? Are you becoming an active learner, not just a passive "patient"?

Do you begin to understand how you have organized experience into categories which arbitrarily exclude other interpretations or possibilities? For instance, what do you fear, and to what extent are those fears useful? to what extent excessive? Or, what do you want that you haven't admitted, and how can you explore these desires?

It is worth noting that many aspects of psychotherapy can also be practiced as a collaborative inquiry into material from "the other", such as dreams or emotionally charged experiences. This practice can be carried out in a variety of contexts. Much can be learned from discussions of imaginative literature, from groups that study their dreams together, from journal-keeping classes, and the like.

Also, it needs to be said that therapy is not "psychology" any more than religion is spirituality, or than school is education. Therapy offers access to understanding how the principles of psychology are working in our lives, but what matters is our handling of this and other psychological information. The living study of psychology is the mindful enterprise of taking what is learned about the Other from whatever sources, and integrating that into the way we relate to the world in our everyday living.

Nine

Philosophy & the Occult:

knowledge of the Other

Where spirituality and psychology aim at encountering, and being affected by, the Other, there is a contrasting approach with its own lengthy history. This other "way" has as its intent to minimize the subjective human response, striving instead to *know* the Other by the disciplined use of reason. The object is to understand the nature of reality not from sensory and common-sense experience, but in accordance with special principles derived by reason and insight.

One version of this approach is metaphysical philosophy. Literally, metaphysics means "above physics", a logical inquiry into the "laws" that must be in effect to make the perceivable world operate as it does. While physics (and science generally) deals only with theories which can be rigorously tested, and with quantifiable information that can be observed repeatedly, metaphysics is a logical speculation about universal order.

An example of a physical hypothesis would be the law of gravity. Isaac Newton formulated this principle to explain why objects fall down instead of up. Before reaching its final form, this hypothesis was tested with a large variety of objects in carefully controlled situations of many kinds. Then the results were written as a mathematical formula that expressed the observed results of the "power of attractions between" the objects in question.

(We might note here that Einstein's Theory of Special Relativity explains the phenomenon of falling objects in a completely different way, although mathematically the relationships are nearly identical to Newton's. This tells us that physical "laws" are primarily a matter of convenience, not reality: we use them as long as they work.)

In contrast to scientific hypothesizing, when metaphysical philosophers discuss the relationships of "things that exist" with "principles that order and control these things", they are speculating based on their free-ranging experience (not laboratory experiments) and their use of logic (not mathematical expression of controlled observation of particular events.)

In the Middle Ages, St. Thomas Aquinas gave proofs of the existence of God, attempting to demonstrate by logic that there must be an ordering principle prior to, and in control of, the existence of the physical universe. On the other hand, the twentieth century thinker Jean Paul Sartre insisted on the logic of accepting that unordered existence came before meaningful order. (This philosophical stance he called "existentialism", which says that there is no natural order intrinsic to life, but rather order is imposed by us as—and because—we need it.)

Which is right? We can look at the evidence each philosopher marshals, at the logic he uses. We can check our personal experience for examples that don't seem to conform with the philosophies presented. We can ask which system seems to explain more about the nature of Being as we understand it. But there is no laboratory where we can test "Being", no philosophical prediction that can be conclusively proven or disproven in a particular situation, no predictable application. So metaphysical philosophy is ultimately a matter of belief based on logic, religion without the spiritual aspect. It is an attempt to describe objectively how everything is related, and that attempt includes positioning human experience as no more nor less important than other experiences.

Metaphysical philosophy appeals to the abstract forms of logical necessity for its validity (e.g. if all humans are mammals, and I am a human, then I must be a mammal) rather than appealing to subjective, intuitive rightness. In this way it tries to remove itself from the peculiar biases and accidents of emotion, and from the untrustworthiness of our senses. Insofar as most of us are tossed and turned by emotion, metaphysical speculation is a useful antidote—a way of coolly considering how we may be part of the scheme of things, in perspectives we normally don't "see."

The concept of time can be used to illustrate this kind of thinking. We all have a sure, common-sense notion of what time is; but we have all experienced how clock time is different from subjective time e.g. how you can look up after what seemed moments reading an absorbing book and find it is well past midnight, or conversely how a deep nap that seemed an eternity took only moments. We know, also, that children tend to experience time as durations (from breakfast to play-outside-time, from going-to-school to coming-home-time), not as measured intervals of minutes and hours. Which kind of time is "real"?

Perhaps we think of calendar time as more straightforward. There are seven days to a week, four weeks to a month, twelve months to a year. But then we find that a "year" is a measure of time based on the re-appearance of an object in the sky, and differs slightly depending on which celestial marker is used. We also may be aware that the number of months in a year is arbitrary—the Romans had ten 30-day months, then added two more to keep the months from running ahead of the season as a 300-day year would cause. Actually, we could just as well have a calendar based on ten 35-day months, or whatever combination we deemed convenient.

Knowing this, it still took me by surprise to learn that in some countries the new year and the seasons are associated with times other than the ones I was used to (e.g. winter in the southern hemisphere corresponds to our summer); and even that in some traditional societies the "week" can be other than seven days. (I remember reading with wonderment about an African society that had 3-day "weeks" to measure the cycle between market days.)

It was Einstein, of course, who compounded this confusion by telling us that time is "relative" not only subjectively but also objectively. According to his calculations, someone travelling close to the speed of light, say in a space ship travelling away from earth, would be subject to time differently than someone on the planet. If the ship were going 99% of the speed of light, the person would age only one year for every seven that passed on earth.

With all this information to digest, "time" becomes a much less graspable notion than first appeared. We can still use our simple ideas in most everyday transactions, just as we can still use Newton's concept of gravity; but we have to realize that we use them because they work well enough for usual needs, not because they are "true".

Thus "time" enters the realm of the metaphysical, as the questions we ask take us from our everyday way of experiencing. This kind of questioning may seem useless, impractical, downright obstructionist. In fact, some 200 years ago, in responding to a metaphysical theory put forth by one Lord Berkeley, that "objects" exist only as the perceptions of others, Samuel Johnson (a well-known man of letters) loudly and painfully kicked a chair while exclaiming something like, "I refute it thus!" Yet now we "know" that all there is is "matter" made of energy in more-or-less stable configurations, and we can "choose" to pay attention to the changeable aspects of the relationships rather than the stable ones.

For instance, we can see—and use— a wooden "chair" as flammable material, or as a pattern of pieces that can be re- arranged otherwise; or, we can realize that if we show a chair to someone who has never seen one, someone who perhaps has only sat on mats on the ground, that such a person would have no idea what he was looking at. The chair exists *as a chair* only as an idea that many people share...that is, as a shared perception, just as Lord Berkeley had said.

Some ideas are common (chairs), many less so (ghosts). Some seem universal (Jung's archetypes) such as Mother and Father. But in any case, where do they come from? and are they "real"? is there an objective reality or just ideas and perceptions? How do reality, ideas, perception all relate, and where do we fit into this relating?

With questions like these, metaphysical philosophy goes one step above whatever has been formulated, asking where that so-called final formulation came from and if it is logically acceptable. In the eighteenth century, when David Hume speculated that even the basis of logic itself must be so questioned, he almost drove himself mad. And when Einstein showed that Newtonian physics was just a useful way of doing business, not a reflection of reality, he moved physics into a metaphysical framework that upset the intellectual (and some say spiritual) balance of the Western world. (In fact, radical questioning of "science" as a kind of knowledge and procedure has gone hand-in-hand with experiments based on Einstein's theories; and fascinating new notions have been raised, such as the thought that the only thing science can reveal is the success and the limits of the human perceptual/logical system; or that the true "matter" of scientific inquiry is the spiritual ambiguity of human understanding.)

While metaphysical speculating may seem simply an idle or unnerving exercise far from the meat-and-potatoes of life, there is little doubt that it has added another dimension to the possible understanding of ourselves and the Other. For those with interest, there is another approach to these concerns through study of the esoteric and occult. Until quite recently, educated members of "modern civilization" have tended to view these systems and practices as superstitious leftovers from the unenlightened past, with no logical or scientific basis, as they deal with powers that could not be measured by the five senses, or by any known instruments. Their forms and relations were codified centuries ago, and people who have called themselves privy to the "mysteries" have typically been viewed as being a little crazed, if not ungodly.

In the last few decades, occult systems have regained some credibility from a variety of factors, and have begun to be integrated into common, acceptable ways of thinking. Without having to believe in them as "true", they present a means of relating to the material of our lives in a way that often proves as useful as scientifically testable hypotheses. For this reason, I would like to take brief note of some of them.

One group of beliefs and practices is based on the relationships among the heavenly bodies and the way they affect human life. In simple forms, this wisdom begins with the myths concerning the seasons, the sun, moon, planets and stars. Astrology is a complicated system of analysis based on ancient interpretation of the meaning of celestial relationships, and long history of pragmatic observations. Astrologers claim to be able to determine the most important influences on an individual's character and history by diagramming the location and inter-relations of the planets, stars and zodiacal zones at time of birth. They then speculate on how this original configuration "transits" through time, that is, enters into new relationships as the celestial bodies continue to change position.

Another mystical system has to do with the significance of numbers and forms. Artists have long been aware of the aesthetic power of the basic geometrical shapes (circle, triangle, square, circle, etc.) The art and architecture of religions abound in spheres and pyramids, ovals, pentangles and spirals. Some of Bach's greatest music is said to be based on numerical proportions.

Numerology is a related branch of study that assigns meaning to each of the numbers from 1 to 10, and explores the hidden significance and power of various numerical relationships. One aspect of the Kabbala (an early book of mystical knowledge studied by traditional Jews) relates the numbers to the letters of the Hebrew alphabet, suggesting that every word (especially in the first books of the Old Testament) is a code for the numerical relations expressed by the order of its letters.   Another group of studies is based on beliefs that colors and materials and life-forms give off unique vibrations; and that some people, with extra-sensitive "receiving" equipment (such as psychics, clairvoyants, and telepaths) are able to detect these vibrations, work with them and interpret them. There is also a belief that the whole universe is awash in vibrations and harmonics, that the old notion of "the music of the spheres" and of "achieving harmony with the world" are not merely metaphors.

Many systems of belief indicate that a non-material aspect of the individual exists, separable from the physical body. People claim to experience "astral projection" where their consciousness leaves the body and is present elsewhere. They are often able to report on events distant in time or space that would seem impossible for them to know about. This aspect of the person may also be the foundation of beliefs in life after death, whether it be the expectation for the "soul" to be re-incarnated in another body, left still attached to earth but without a body (e.g. as a ghost or ancestral spirit), or set free to participate in another higher form of existence such as in heaven or nirvana.

There are also health or spiritual practices based on non-western ideas of anatomy which locate non-material organs, energy centers and pathways within the body. These very specific "sciences" have derived treatments involving positioning and movement and mental exercises (examples are yoga and the martial arts) or by healing interventions such as acupuncture or shiatsu massage.

These practices all teach the quieting and focussing of the mind as requisite to better perceiving the guiding voices of Universal Forces, and to unblocking natural physiological responses such as breathing, blood circulation and the dispersion or concentration of life-force (energy.)

Another kind of healing practice, known to so-called primitive civilizations, involves the use of chant and dance, herbs, sacred objects, animals spirits and the like. These "magical" practices enable shamans and medicine people and witches to have access to forces beyond the realm of our five senses and physical bodies for the purpose of curing physical, psychological and even sociological ailments.

Also there are practices designed to disclose the occult reality, analogous to psychotherapeutic techniques for disclosing the unconscious. These include such means as the use of rocks, Tarot cards, palmistry, and the throwing of lots, like the I Ching. There are also metaphysical philosophies such as the Chinese understanding of Yin and Yang (the relation of opposites), the Yogic knowledge of India and the Buddhism of Tibet, all of which describe the universal order in ways markedly different from Western descriptions.

Students and practitioners of these sciences and arts have demonstrated the existence of forces and systems beyond those accounted for by the identified body of knowledge of "Western Civilization." It was no accident that, just when the scientists of the turn-of-the-century Victorian world thought they knew just about all there was to know about the physical world, exploration of minor-seeming discrepancies resulted in the overturn of the Newtonian model of physical reality by the discoveries and theories of the Einsteinian age.

Since that time, modern science has begun to shed light on many of the mysteries that once were called occult. We now, for instance, casually accept the "existence" (that is to say the effects) of gamma-rays, atomic energy, bio-feedback systems, bio-rhythm charts and many other phenomena that 50 years ago would have been considered nonsense.

Additionally, strange energy fields have been photographed around psychic healers. Kirlian photography shows up fields around all living things that seem related to the colored "auras" some psychic claim to see. Scientific studies indicate that the moon's effect is not just physical (as in affecting the tides) but manifold: the idea of the lunatic (from the Latin word "luna" meaning moon) seems to have statistical validity, according to studies that suicides and other psychologically-motivated events vary according to phases of the moon.

Acupuncture (based on China's esoteric anatomy system) is found effective as therapy and anaesthesia, and is being incorporated into Western medicine. Psychedelic drug experiences are scientifically verified as giving access to information that the experimental subject would not be expected to have. And the list goes on.

In a way, this verification of occult knowledge by science is only fair, for science is itself derived from studies in alchemy and esoteric philosophies. And what is verified is that our body of knowledge is smaller, and more faulty , than we like to believe. I would go so far as to conclude, in fact, that rejecting the great storehouse of wisdom available through the teachings of the older traditions leaves us in dangerous ignorance.

It seems also clear, though, that The Identified (i.e. the scientifically established) and the Other (as revealed by occult practices) are not antagonists; and that the purpose of exploring The Other is not to supplant or reduce the Identified. Rather the aim is for the two to encounter each other, for some kind of supernatural or spiritual intercourse to take place.

The approaches sketched out in this chapter suggest ways to initiate this process on an individual basis. There are numerous institutions which can assist: religions, therapies, schools of esoteric arts, academic research of parapsychology; study groups following the teachings of individual spiritual mentors such as Gurdjieff, Krishnamurti and Rudolf Steiner; yoga or martial arts centers, to name a few. Yet as always, the real work is left up to us as individuals, to look for what strongly summons our attention, to take in what is enlarging and strengthening, and to put what is learned to use in our daily living.

We each can come to understand more about our existence— that in many ways we are not who we think we are; that our tasks in life are not defined only by the individuals and social forces that initially shape our conscious minds. We can come to sense our limits and respect the rate of learning appropriate for us.

We can also value the bit of order we create out of the seeming chaos around us—as long as we remember it is a "temporary structure." For we do well to prepare for a time when our castles of confidence and accomplishment will be swept away. We will all experience spiritual crisis, times when we are called on to go *beyond* the presumptions that seemed to serve us well for a while. Our knowledge and beliefs do not so much fail as simply prove inadequate or inaccurate, and we can fortify ourselves for this inevitability.

To my mind, the key here is self-respect complemented by openness and receptivity. When we encounter things we don't understand, even things we disapprove of, we can be open to the learning made possible in the encounter. We can oppose without rejecting, and we can accept without embracing fully. We can strive to retain our integrity while giving up some of what has come into our "possession": material things, relationships, ideas, beliefs.

A turning point along these lines occurred for me during my first year at college. A classmate whose warmth and generosity made her an appreciated friend was reported to have taken part in a fraternity sex-party. I was disturbed. My upbringing and personal uncertainties urged me to repudiate acquaintance with her. Yet another voice arose: "The qualities you like in her are still there. Believe in her." It was a brief but deep crisis, a conflict between charity and judgment. The resolution (which kept my heart open without denying her possible lapse in behavior) was a significant act of freedom.

As we learn better to balance such paradoxical impulses, we enter directly into some kind of transformational process. Paradox: to accept ourselves as responsible for the welfare of less capable beings around us, and responsible for the effects of our actions despite our ignorance of what we do. Paradox: accepting the reciprocal nature of power, as in the old fable of the elephant and the mouse. (An elephant saves a mouse from drowning, then laughs when the mouse says, "I'll pay you back some day." And then comes a time when the size and particular qualities of the mouse are needed to save the elephant.) Sometimes we may seem to be the elephant, sometimes the mouse, but the crucial factor is not which role we play but the quality of respectfulness we bring to the relating.

So...open-mindedness, curiosity, respect, integrity; ability to endure periods of painful confusion fruitfully; willingness to give over, for a time, to the guidance of another discipline in order to build a new "temporary structure", a new working philosophy: these are the chief qualities needed for encountering the Other.

We are going to encounter it anyway, so really the only choice is, do we prepare for it or do we let ourselves be caught off-guard and out-of-shape?

Epilogue:
Whole-Person Living

In the previous chapters we have looked at several aspects of life separately. This finale will offer thoughts on how to deal with the whole—how to locate ourselves and proceed with living with as much vigor, intelligence, fortitude and humor as possible. Or, put another way, how can we live whole-heartedly when everything seems so complicated?

There are a few basic principles that appear to underlie all the detailed analysis in the preceding pages. This chapter will try to bring these to the foreground and elaborate on each.

There is no pretension to be offering here a "solution" to life's problems...only a wish to present my cumulative understanding at this point of time. The hope is to add to what others know, and to help them present (i.e., live) what they know, as best they can.

The first principle I identify is this: things are never what they seem.

We have already questioned the absolute existence of "things", having looked at the notion that a "thing" is as much a collective idea as a being-in-itself. We have also seen that our perceptions (the "seeming" of the principle) are limited: quite literally by the defined range of our knowledge and senses, and more generally in the selective attitudes and conceptions through which we perceive. Both ways, there is something out there beyond what there seems to any of us to be.

We have also observed that we are part of what we experience—we are not invisible, non-participant, objective observers. The positions or postures we assume are only more obtrusive or less, have more or less direct impact on the situation being assessed. In other words, all we know is filtered and shaped by the medium of ourselves and our particular minds.

Also we have concluded that our interpretation of a situation is just one of many possible interpretations; and, in fact, the "situation" in part consists of the differing interpretations of it. So, even should one interpretation satisfy all the "facts" at hand, the existence of another interpretation in itself means the situation is unresolved. The picture in one person's (or one group's) mind never suffices alone to describe anything but itself.

We also know that our understanding of a situation is subject to change. New facts come to light, we discover other angles of looking, other faculties to look with; time and distance give a different perspective.

For instance, I remember going to visit my high school in New York City twenty years after graduation. As the subway train I was on grew closer to the destination, images and recollections flooded me, but experienced very differently than in the past. Certain people I had liked moderately at a distance I now felt a surge of hidden affection for. Others

I had scorned appeared worthy of compassion—or even curiosity. Teachers who had seemed awesome re-appeared as quite human—some admirably so, others regrettably or capriciously so. And above all, I experienced that fierce, scared, straining, somehow hopeful youngster I had been: and felt on one hand sadness that he had spent so many years in such inner loneliness; and on the other, gladness since all his work and errors and trials were essential to the understanding I was now graced with.

And more. As I got off the train and walked silently up the hill to the school campus, a part of that boy's unexpressed potential, trapped then in inexperience and fear, was somehow being redeemed. What I had lived through—miserable as it often had felt—now was transformed. It was not what it had seemed, it had been waiting the proper time to become poignant, beautiful.

A second principle: one of the chief tasks of life is to continue going beyond "what seems" (or more likely, "what has seemed so till now") in whatever ways present themselves to our interest, or impress themselves by threatening our equilibrium.

The importance of this task may be expressed as a pragmatic directive for success ("know the score"); as a moral imperative ("know what you are doing, take responsibility for your actions"); as a philosophical ideal ("know thyself"); as a means to psychological stability or physical health or spiritual transcendence ("know The Way").

But whichever approaches are taken, it is clear that "knowing" in itself is at least as important as "knowing how"...that knowledge of one's place in the scheme of things is needed to complement the technology of survival and accomplishment.

Principle three: my external situation—the domestic, work, social, political circumstances that call forth response from me—is not the result of my willed action (even including my "unconscious" willing.) There are many forces at work, and many possible ways to understand these forces.

It is helpful to examine how "I" as currently conceived of have contributed to shaping the situation and can affect it. But it is equally important to begin studying the other currents at work until such time as they begin to make sense as part of my Other—until I discover how I relate to them and can affect them. Thus as I study the *living* (as opposed to academic) fields of history, sociology, political economy, etc., that is as I come to understand what goes into the making of events and trends in the larger world—I can begin to find possibilities for responding to and entering into the larger realms of social existence.

(I differentiate "living study" from "academic study" in this way: living study is taken on from interest or involvement rather than from impersonal assignment. Academic study may be part of an individual's means of living study, or may lead someone into living study, but many students enrolled in schools are not prepared to engage in study through the intellect alone. That would be fine...except that they may then mistakenly think that there is no other kind of study than one dry and distant from felt significance.

So, yes there is a need for us to find out in some systematic way how different individuals, sensibilities, cultures, intellectual disciplines describe the world. Yet equally there is a need to inquire how this information relates to the world as described by our own culture, family and individual experience. The quest for significance and relationship is the study essential to whole-person living.)

Principle four: The situation I find myself in also has different alternative interpretations. There are, so to speak, several different kinds of stories I can consider myself part of: comedies, tragedies, romances, melodramas, soap operas, allegories, myths, imitations of biblical or historical or literary scenarios. Similarly, any of the various aspects discussed in earlier chapters may be at the fore at a given time, and then the focus may shift to another. This diversity and changeability suggests, for starters, the wisdom of not fixing on any one possibility too intently.

For instance, sometimes life seems to have forward, progressive direction—we want to go from here to there and we arrive. Sometimes we see only repetition, patterns re-appearing in thin disguise. Sometimes there seems to be only random happenstance, with no meaning except what we impose in the face of what the existential philosophers call "the absurd." Sometimes it appears as if a purposeful mockery of our intentions and beliefs is being enacted. Sometimes there seems to be a higher order that we can only guess at, which dwarfs our own efforts at "meaningful action" yet which can be felt guiding us along a proper way.

One or another of these modes may predominate in our thinking for periods of time; but most of us experience all of them, if only as fleeting thoughts, as shadowy questions that afflict our confidence.

Or, we may be aware of several of these modes as possible simultaneously, and become confused at having to choose one to live by, to make decisions by. This perplexity can escalate to anxiety when, say, we are told by one authority that our mortal souls depend on our obedience to what we have been taught; and by another that our success in rising above the mass of pitiable mediocrity depends on our not remaining swaddled in conventional morality.

In my understanding, the most important concern here is not the decision but the anxiety. We can begin to penetrate the clouds of confusion only by a willingness to endure uncertainty with our minds and senses kept open. We can prepare ourselves to accept the inevitability of partial error, to make amends for whatever damage we inadvertently do, to learn from our miscalculations. We can learn to live with paradox while we slowly adjust beliefs piecemeal to assimilate new evidence. New understanding can grow out of our old, imperfect ones in a natural way: we do not have to convert or willfully transform ourselves into someone else.

Beyond this, I can only counsel against fanaticism. It is no individual's responsibility to establish a universal belief system. Yet we may find a way to express cogently the learning of our education and experience, as long as we understand that these expressions are imperfect. No matter how strongly our beliefs are "true" for us, our formulations remain inexact and inadequate.

So we need the competitive jostling of other beliefs to test our own by. We can allow our beliefs to be modified—strengthened by confirming experience or altered by contrary evidence. We can grant the stimulating effect of others with differing beliefs when both theirs and ours are maintained with modesty and (better yet) good humor. And we can see that most important of all is the willingness to entertain contrary beliefs and contrary evidence rather than dogmatically excluding one's own beliefs from question.

The last principle is the ultimate importance of breathing freely and of giving attention as generously, spontaneously, unconditionally and democratically as possible.

I've sometimes thought that most of our actions and attributes are matters of reflex, natural process, social conditioning and chance. Our "personality" seems certainly to be composed mainly of the interplay among these elements—somehow not truly our own.

Yet I find a small channel of free will emerging from breath and attention. Accordingly, our independent "selves" grow and become effective in two ways. First, through the practice of "purposeless breathing", when attention is narrowed as closely as possible to the breath itself, or broadened so it remains unfixed on anything. Second, through paying unconditional attention to others. This requires us to detach our taking in of perceptions from the need to process them immediately, that is from the need to evaluate and react to them...taking them on their terms, for their sake.

By these two kinds of practice, a Mind may be created, joining intellect, sensing and reflex—a Mind capable of spacious understanding beyond knowing, of responding rather than reacting. As this Mind becomes larger and stronger, it is able to give of itself...give its attention and its life breath... to the world it exists in.

Our breath (our simple presence) and our undivided attention (with few or no hopes, desires, goals attached) seem to me the dearest gifts we can offer. Yet our ability to locate these, and offer them straightforwardly, requires pure and constantly renewed intent.

May we be blessed with the wherewithal to stay resolute in this undertaking.

Postscript

This manuscript represents a summation of much of my experience and thinking till now. It is an offering; yet it is also an invitation to response. For the response will be the means—the impulse, the material, the circulating energy—to sustain the continued work (and play) of whole-person living.

Your challenges, affirmations, inquiries, communications of any sort, are solicited and welcome. You may write to me directly at my post box, 164 N. Blackstone Ave., Ste. 1445, Fresno, CA 93701.